Mazie's MOUNTAIN

Living a Spirited Life With a Disability

by
Dr. Carman Wiese
Mazie Petree

Petree & Wiese Publishing

Petree & Wiese Publishing

P. O. Box 1422
Sealy, Texas 77474

Designed by Jack Petree
Illustrations by Mary Ellen Petree

ISBN: 0-9716390-0-0

First printing / January 2002

Additional copies of this book are available for *$20.00 (US)
US/Canada delivery: Add $3.95 for shipping and handling,
add $1.00 for each additional book.
Texas residents: Add $1.55 sales tax per book (7 3/4%)
Only checks or money orders accepted.

Petree & Wiese Publishing
P. O. Box 1422
Sealy, Texas 77474
e-mail: sales@maziesmountain.com
www.maziesmountain.com

*Prices subject to change without notice

Printed in the United States by:
Morris Publishing
3212 East Highway 33 • Kearney, NE 68847
1-800-650-7888

BIOGRAPHY

WRITER: Dr. Carman Wiese
                B.S. Texas Woman's University
                M.Ed Houston Baptist University
                Ed.D Grambling State University
                Taught in public and parochial elementary school
                Retired from Southwest Texas Junior College
                Presently managing family home medical business

When asked to write *Mazie's Mountain*, she felt that having grown up with Mazie, her years of teaching and her empathetic personality are such that she could help get the depth and sincerity of the message in *Mazie's Mountain* across to a wide audience.

Carman Wiese
HCR 3 Box 5 Quail Run II
Del Rio, Texas 78840
e-mail: carman@maziesmountain.com

Mazie Petree
P. O. Box 1422
Sealy, Texas 77474
e-mail: mazie@maziesmountain.com

WebSite: www.maziesmountain.com

ACKNOWLEDGMENTS

I would like to give thanks to God for sending me my support system. I have relied on Him throughout my life. It is said God will not place His people where they do not belong although society may place a person where he or she should not be. God knew the family I needed. He placed me with a mother and father, Neal and Louise Shaver, who would understand me and my needs. God did not stop there.

He gave me a loving and supporting husband, Jack Petree. Then He blessed Jack and me with a son, Daniel. Along with all of these blessings, He sent me many friends. My friends have been the family I have "picked up" along the way. It is to these people that I owe a debt of gratitude for all the things I have been able to accomplish. I am proud to say that I cherish the life God planned for me. Last, but not least, God provided a deep enduring friend in Carman Parker Wiese. Without her, this book would have never been written.

Chapter 1

THE LAST CHAPTER

I know, this should be entitled "THE FIRST CHAPTER," but I wrote it to be the last chapter. However, Carman insisted that it be the first chapter because it is a synopsis of what you will read about in *Mazie's Mountain*. By reading this chapter you will gain an understanding of my point of view and the message—an example of what God can do.

Writing *Mazie's Mountain* reveals many of my frustrations in having to prove myself over and over again. One obstacle I still have trouble with is getting a job. Presently, I have applied for two jobs. One job is as an activity director for a day program. The other is as an office assistant in a one- woman office. When I see others in society, whose abilities are inferior to mine, being given a chance at a job, for which I applied and was turned down, I am livid! This is very difficult for me. The workforce tends to shut the door. It doesn't slam—that would be against the law. But, it is shut nevertheless.

The doubt, as to whether or not I can do a job, is still held by society. It is there because of my "disability." I speak intelligently and I am knowledgeable on many topics. However,

1

my speech is strained. I write. It is hard to read. I type. It is not up to speed and I use the fingers that are natural for me. I walk. A normal gait, but at times unsteady. Get the picture? This may be the mountain the work force cannot or will not remove. During interviews I get, " You do not fit all of our criteria." or "You are an inspiration and you have such energy. Keep checking back. Something may open up."

My ability is there. I have shown it by taking care of my husband, my home, and myself. I also helped raise a son. I have worked in various organizations and have taken care of Momma when she was ill. I've owned and operated my own business.

This is the fear my Daddy had some 36 years ago. So it really has not changed. That is our society! I may never be able to be in the workforce in order to earn a living.

My only salvation is my belief in God. He understands. He has provided me with determination. He has provided me with my support system. God knows what I can and cannot do better than I know. I have to tell myself that maybe it is not my lot in life to be in the workforce. I am grateful that Jack is patient and understanding about the insurmountable obstacle that has not disappeared from the workforce. As with many husbands, he would not mind at all if I were able to take some of the financial pressure off of him and help pay some bills.

Oh, I can volunteer all I want. I am told, "You are an inspiration to others." So, I ask myself, "Is this what God uses me for? Should I be satisfied with this?"

We are all on a journey. The journey is different for each of us. Through my journey I have felt alone at times in my disabilities. Not because I was physically alone but emotionally alone. People see when I cannot control my shakes, unable to hide my facial grimaces or when I speak with a stressful speech pattern. My support system has been there to comfort and help me through many of these trying times. However, emotionally, no one can possibly understand, but God. God knows every feeling and thought. Now THAT is scary!

When life becomes difficult it is essential to be quiet, still and patient. It is during these difficult times that I call on the Lord. He is always there—for me and for you. Jesus had a lonely life. People did not understand Him at times. He would go off to meditate when He was troubled about what lay ahead of Him. It was when He was alone that God explained what He was to do or accomplish next. God would show Him which path He should take and what He was to teach His people. At times, Jesus' disciples did not understand what was expected of them. He taught them to trust and believe. I believe. I believe that God will always tell us how to go and which way to go. We only have to listen.

Throughout *Mazie's Mountain*, I show the mountain or what seems to be a mountain range I have encountered within my journey. The mountain has obstacles—peaks and valleys. I have had God in my life and He has provided a support system. I believe each of us needs a support system—one being God and the other being those whom God has provided. Through the use of these supports, I have learned what I can accomplish. I am forever grateful because without them I would be lost. I feel I have conveyed this attitude to others and was gratified when Jenelle, a friend from my church in Alief wrote, "I knew when I met her she was a very special person. Strong in her beliefs in God, herself, and her family."

Situations in which we encounter those who are different or those who are disabled sadden me. I have worked with the disabled. I have taken them out to eat, to ballgames, sightseeing, etc. When working with those who are handicapped or disabled I forget they appear different. I forget that their speech is loud or unusual. (I guess I am classified "disabled" since my speech pattern would fit into this category.) There could be and have been tense situations—being out in the community with them. Once, my "disabled" friends and I were confronted and asked to leave an establishment. I was told, "If you can't help from making a spectacle with your party, please leave." It seemed a customer had approached the manager of this particular establishment. The customer did not want us (the disabled) around his children. This is sooooo sad! The customer did not want to take the time to talk with his children and discuss the fact that not all people are created alike. Possibly, the adult was the one uncomfortable, not the children.

I have been in similar situations while on a plane and another while attending a social event. Once a flight attendant asked, "Are you all right?" I said, "Sure." Then I tried to practice one of my relaxation exercises where I would try to forget I had a left side. Have you ever tried to forget about your entire left side? When I can really concentrate and can relax, the tremors stop.

I recently attended a church conference. I looked out, over the crowd, and noticed there were no individuals at the conference who appeared to be handicapped. Out of those thousands of people in attendance, was I the only one singing in a stressed voice? Oh well, somewhere it does say to "make a joyful noise." That is what I was doing! Of course, those who were sitting near me might not agree.

My point is—God makes us different. He gives us different figures, facial features, abilities or talents and disabilities. Our talents must be used. I believe my talent is perseverance. So, this is my motto: Go for it! God knows! He knows my limitations and my gifts.

If we have a problem, we can stew about it and be depressed, or like climbing a mountain, take it in stride and climb out or over it!

Chapter 2

Be bold. Do not be afraid.
Ask for help on your journey through life.

When, I sat down to think about how to describe my life, I immediately thought of a mountain---with its valleys and peaks. The highs and lows seemed to relate to the emotional highs and lows of my life. But life is more than just the emotions. There is the physical side of life. The more I thought and the more I wrote, the more I began to see myself soaring with my life's accomplishment. I was like a bird soaring, but hey, I wasn't going to be just any bird, soaring through life. I am special—I had to be an eagle!

I have always had a dream to tell my story. This story is a tale of achieving life's goals in spite of the mountain and valleys of living life with a physical handicap. I feel fortunate that my undiagnosed cerebral palsy has not been a barricade for me. Although it has been a hindrance, it has never stopped me from achieving my goals. I have always had the support system that is needed even by those who are considered to be "normal." My support was just more visible and tangible.

After my father died, my brother Steve, and I were going through Daddy's papers. I came across Daddy's scrapbook. Looking through this book of remembrance, I saw no pictures or articles about me. Page after page was filled with pictures of Steve—Steve's junior high exploits as an athlete, his high school and college athletic honors, and his being drafted by the Houston Oilers. My heart was torn. In anguish, I cried, "There's nothing in here about me!"

I was devastated. I was "Daddy's girl," but he didn't have any scrapbook of me! Steve put his arm around me and said, "Daddy was just as proud of you and your accomplishments as anything that I have ever done." At that moment those were the words I needed to hear. His words and strong arm at that most vulnerable time reflected his deep down love, compassion, and understanding for me. Steve, the big, tough jock! The tear in my heart, from the loss of my dear daddy, began to mend.

This book is for those who have "handicaps" or are perceived to have "handicaps" and for those who are the heart of our lives—the support system. A SUPPORT SYSTEM IS A VITAL PART TO BEING WHO YOU CAN BE! I know it was and is for me. Without this support system life is difficult for even the "normal" person. This support system can be in the form of Divine Guidance, immediate family, friends, co-workers, acquaintances, professionals, or membership in a professional support system.

I don't think I've led a spectacular or even exemplary life. But, my life has been interesting. It has been full of wonderful, exciting moments of high emotional excitement and I hope there are many of these mountain peaks yet to come. It has also contained heartbreaks and heartaches so profound that the climb from the deepest valley of despair and humiliation seemed insurmountable. I can only hope that the worst of these are over, but knowing if that is not the case, God is with me and has given me my support system to be able to endure.

Of course, just like real life, concerning the day in and day out living, I could not accomplish this task of writing about my life alone. Once I made up my mind to undertake this process, I knew I had to have help. So, I asked my family, friends and acquaintances to write about how they came to know me; what they remember about the relationship we've had or continue to have. But most important, I wanted to know how they feel about this relationship. (I never have liked to ask easy questions, heh, heh, heh!)

I wanted the good, the bad, the ugly, the happy—as usual, I wanted it all, "the whole truth and nothing but the truth"—from their perspective, of course. Since this is my book and it may be the only time I might have a "captive audience" I have decided to throw in a few little "words of wisdom." You might call them that or you might call them "words to live by" or better yet, "words of faith and encouragement." But, they are definitely words by which I live.

Chapter 3

Life: Mine in a nutshell....

It was a dark and stormy night.... No, that's not right. OK I'll begin again.

It was the best of times; it was the worst of times.... Nooooo, I can't use that either. But, in reality "it was the best of times, it was the worst of times" does describe my life.

I am Mary Anna (Mazie) Shaver Petree born in Palestine, Texas on January 14, 1945. I have to take my parent's word on this since I really can't remember that far back. My first recollections are of life in Eagle Lake, Texas. I didn't spend all of my life there. I lived in Houston, Texas and graduated from Westbury High School in 1964. From there I moved to Huntsville, Texas and attended Sam Houston State University 1964 to 1968. After I married John Michael (Jack) Petree on August 3, 1968 we moved back to Houston and lived there a number of years, even after the birth of our son, Daniel. We now reside in Sealy, Texas.

Thus far the information and the milestones of my life I've presented don't sound greatly different than the majority of other people's information and milestones. However, I believe I have a unique perspective on life and living because I have the characteristics of someone with cerebral palsy. I don't mean to brag about it or complain about it; I'm just stating a fact. Most people don't know what cerebral palsy is or even understand the characteristics of one who has cerebral palsy.

The following definition is taken from the Internet. The sources of the definition are the National Information Center for Children and Youth with Disabilities and the Ontario Federation for Cerebral Palsy. You can find each of these by typing in "cerebral palsy" and let your search engine go to work for you.

Cerebral palsy is a condition caused by damage to the brain, usually occurring before, during or shortly following birth. "Cerebral" refers to the brain and "palsy" to a disorder of movement or posture. It is neither progressive nor communicable. This damage interferes with messages from the brain to the body, and from the body to the brain. Depending on which areas of the brain have been damaged, one or more of the following may occur: (1) muscle tightness or spasms, (2) involuntary movement, (3) difficulty with "gross motor skills" such as walking or running, (4) difficulty with "fine motor skills" such as writing or doing up buttons, and (5) difficulty in perception and sensation.

My definition is a little different. I say that it is an "affliction" (and I call it that because it was inflicted upon me; I can certainly assure you that I did not choose to have it!) that causes people to look at me as if I am mentally retarded or mentally handicapped because I shimmy and shake, and my voice quivers and quakes. *Of course that does put those with cerebral palsy and who are ambulatory at an advantage when it comes to certain dance steps that were popular when I was growing up.*

The medical definition for cerebral palsy (CP) is: a neuromuscular dysfunction that occurs early in childhood as a result of injury to the brain before, during, or after birth.

The form of cerebral palsy of which I have the characteristics is athetoid cerebral palsy. This is the palsy in which the affected parts of the body perform involuntary writhing movements. Turning, twisting, and facial grimacing are characterized with jerky, abrupt flailing motions. Those not in the know often take such movements as signs of mental or emotional disturbance. *Just wait until I tell about the diagnosis of the "experts" who should have known this information, as well as about an "Aggie" who asked a really stupid question.*

The most extraordinary thing about my "condition" is that I was not diagnosed as having the characteristics of one having cerebral palsy until I was in my late teens! Can you believe it? All those years I spent being frustrated—trying to follow the dictates of all the so-called specialists. They told me I could "take control" and "you can do it if you try hard enough." I use the term "so-called" as an adjective for the specialists because of the length of time that my CP characteristics were not diagnosed—*19 v e r y l o n g years.*

There's also a flip side to not having been diagnosed as having CP. Maybe I would have given up on myself, or not set any goals or had ambitions for myself. Maybe my parents might have given up on me. This diagnosis would have been a good excuse for everyone to lower their expectations for me, especially my inability to do many things or my difficulty doing some of the most mundane things, such as feeding myself or brushing my hair.

14

An example of my hair dealing days included the time I spent learning to roll my own hair. I was a teenager during the bouffant hair days. This meant ROLLERS! Thank goodness for those ugly, spiky, brush rollers. By using them and creating a "hair nest" and by placing a large hair net over the confused array of rollers, I created my "style." I slept with this "do" every night. I'm sure I was not the only one to suffer through these agonizing nights. I don't know how many others had the type of "array" my tremors helped produce.

This book is written to tell you how my life was and is and continues to be with its mountains and valleys, my mental and physical challenges…. I've got to stop this chattering and get on with it; otherwise, I will lose you right off the bat.

Chapter 4

"It's a girl!"

"All 3 pounds of her" was left unsaid.

Those words began my first impact on the men in my life—my father took one look at me and fainted.

That's how this long journey began. It was a long time before I breathed deeply enough to be able to live. There was no assistance provided to help me breathe deeply. This became my first mountain to climb. It was a long time before my mother was allowed to see me—24 hours. It was a long time before she was allowed to hold me—3 days. But the longest time was the 19 years that passed before I was diagnosed as having the characteristics of one who has cerebral palsy—not being mentally or physically retarded, not emotionally disturbed—but a medical diagnosis.

My birth certificate is unique. Of course, each birth certificate is unique to each individual; mine is even more so. It says, "stillborn." Then, "stillborn" is crossed out and "born alive" is written. I had a pulse and a heartbeat, but the doctor could not detect any breathing because it was so shallow. This is a definite cause and effect situation. Shallow breathing caused a lack of oxygen to the brain; lack of oxygen caused brain cells to die; dead brain cells caused lack of motor skills; lack of motor skills and the reasons for it resulted in what is now called cerebral palsy.

I was welcomed into a warm, loving family. My brother, Steve, is 5 years older than I, and, therefore, I was just a minor blip in his life. *How little he knew*! My mother was a very outgoing person while my daddy was much more reserved. Steve was well—Steve was Steve. Mother had had a normal pregnancy, and although she smoked later in life, she was not a smoker during pregnancy. So if you're thinking smoking contributed to my small birth weight, you are wrong.

Mother was fortunate that she was able to have a practical nurse to help her with me for the first thirty days of my life. While we lived in Palestine, she had help with the housework, too. I'm just telling you about this so you will understand. I was not neglected by my mother because of her housework or any other responsibilities she had. In fact, this may be one of the major reasons my parents were able to pick up so early on my difficulties. I was very small (of course, at my present stage and age and size fourteen instead of a six or eight dress that would be a blessing) and everything (head, arms, legs, etc.) was in proportion. *AHHHH, for that to be true today! Well, although those appendages are still in proportion, the "top" and "bottom" measurements could certainly be better—36-24-36 sounds good!* But, my coordination was poor.

I did not crawl, but scooted on my seat and pushed with my right arm. The right side of my body was the stronger. But, I wanted to grab everything as well as eat with my left hand, although I was less coordinated with this side. This led to many frustrating eating "messes." But, even with all these problems, I still was named Baby Picture of the Week in the <u>Palestine Times</u> when I was one!

I didn't talk until I was two years old, and then I spoke with a speech impediment. My parents took me to specialists in Dallas, Texas. The doctors were no help. They either could not or would not classify my problem.

Over the years, my parents took me to many specialists. I visited neurologists, physical therapists, hearing specialists, as well as general practitioners. I underwent innumerable tests. I was taken to one testing facility to determine whether or not I was mentally able to start first grade. *Can you imagine that!*

Because of my physical "quirks" it had to be determined if I was mentally able to start first grade. Give me a break! It was my limbs that shimmied and shook, not my intelligence!

Anyway, back to the testing. One test went something like this: They gave me about ten verbal commands at one time:

"Get up from your chair. Walk to the back of the room to the door. Walk to the water fountain. Get a drink. Walk back to the door. Turn the doorknob. Open the door. Come into the room. Close the door. Walk to the desk. Pick up the pencil. Write an X on the paper. Place the pencil in the tester's hand. Walk back to your chair. Sit down."

I think most dogs would be able to obey those commands.

Still, my dad was nervous about the tests. He knew there was nothing wrong with my intelligence, but it was a tense, trying situation. OF COURSE I PASSED! Daddy was so relieved. He had this big grin on his face. It was as if he were the one taking the test. But, I DID GOOD!! Such support! He wanted to do the test for me, but let me do it on my own.

That wasn't the end of the testing however. There was more testing for eyesight, fine motor and gross motor skills as well as for IQ. The outcome was that I was ready for school.

Chapter 5

Learn to live with what God gives you—it may take years.

They were the best of times; they were the worst of times. *OOPS, there I go again.* But, can't everyone say that about school years? There were the great, exciting high times and then there were those low, humiliating, lonesome times. I probably had more low times than most people or at least more than most of my peers. Luckily, I probably had more support than many of my peers and most other people.

Continuing with my story, after we left Palestine (where I proudly remind you, that at the ripe old age of one I was named "Baby Picture of the Week"), we moved to Sinton, Texas and then to Eagle Lake, Texas.

Eagle Lake was a great place in which to spend those five years between the ages of five and ten and in which to begin school. When we first arrived, the company my daddy worked for, Tidewater, wanted us to live out in the country next to the plant, in a company house. But, my parents wanted to live in town because my brother was active in sports and they wanted me to have playmates.

It would have been so much easier on my parent's marriage if we had lived next to the plant since Daddy was on call 24 hours a day. But as usual, Mother and Daddy put family first. So, we lived in the only housing available, the Presbyterian parsonage. The parsonage was on the same street where Carman lived. We became best friends and almost inseparable.

After all the testing that I had undergone the only suggestion the doctors gave were for me to take speech therapy. Therefore, Mother enrolled me as a regular summer student in speech therapy at the University of Houston. She did this the year I turned six and before I started first grade. I attended classes Monday, Wednesday, and Friday, two hours each day. I had homework each night. I had poems and sounds to read and practice. I had to make a notebook of pictures, cut from magazines, depicting each sound. Neither my family nor my friends were allowed to help me by cutting out pictures. Also, they were not allowed to give me anything unless I gave the correct pronunciation of the word for the object or service. And boy, did they ever stick to this rule! Carman couldn't understand why she couldn't help me since we always did everything together. In fact, she said,

"I remember your going to Houston and having to come home and make a scrapbook. I was so hurt because I couldn't help you with it. The nerve!!! Of course back then, I didn't understand why. I just knew that we always did everything together and here was something so special and I could not participate."

After about a year and a half, Mother and Daddy bought an older home and remodeled it. The move to the older, bigger house gave me another playmate, John. He lived across the street from our new house. Thank goodness the house was still only two blocks from Carman.

I don't remember too much about my beginning school but the memories I do have include my two best friends Carman and John. Carman is the same age as I (well, a little bit older, but who's counting) and we were in the same classes. John is a year younger and was a grade behind me. Although my "difference" was easily accepted and I had a lot of playmates, I relied on Carman and John to keep me up with everything that was going on in school and in the town. These two playmates are especially cherished. I was at their house or they were at my house. Carman was my interpreter when teachers could not understand me. John was like a little brother to me. He gave me my nickname, Mazie. We played and fought, fought and played. Even after all these years, I can still call them friends.

I remember John and Daddy teaching me to ride a bike. It took me one week of hard work to be able to get on and off my bike without falling. The combination of my lack of coordination and those darn narrow sidewalks were no help. Either Daddy or John could be on one side but not both on each side. Through patience on the part of Daddy and John and many bruises later, I became a successful bike rider. I had wings. I rode all over town.

John and I also played what we then called "little cars." We were into matchbox type cars before matchbox was a household word. We would build forts from old woodpiles or dig deep holes in the ground with tunnels from room to room. I guess I had as much strength as he did because he played with me as if I were another boy. I also remember that John thought I made the best mud pies. I don't know whether or not he remembers, but he actually ate them. Now that is a TRUE friend! Oh for those young, naïve days.

Most people looked at me as just a little girl with a physical problem and as someone trying to live life to the highest potential. By having a family structure as I did, people treated me no differently than any other girl my age.

I also remember that school was not easy for me. It wasn't just the work that was hard for me to keep up with, it was also the social interaction with my peers. I had friends, but I was still the last one to be picked for the teams during recess and the first one to be caught if we played chase or Jail.

While in elementary school, I was always what is now called "mainstreamed." The teachers knew my parents and were usually lenient toward my work habits. If I did not finish a test or my work, I was graded on me—on what I had finished. Although at the time I thought this was great, it later made schoolwork more difficult, because I was getting further and further behind.

Momma signed me up for tap, ballet, and acrobatics with my friends. We participated in dance recitals showing off our prowess. I have to stop here and have Carman's comments about one dance recital inserted here.

> Remember that dance recital where I was to be the "STAR" or rather that was my perception, and I became very ill? Of course, you took my place! I know it wasn't your fault, but that didn't compute, as they say, at the time. I wanted to be the elephant trainer and lead the parade. I really wanted to crack that whip over the elephant, my brother. But NOOOOOO!!!!. You "stole" the show!

Mary, John's mother, was my instructor for tap, ballet and acrobatics. I took twirling also. Alas, this was definitely not my forte! Actually, I was a danger to others with this endeavor! But it was fun.

Here is a portion of the letter that Mary wrote to me about me, about John, and about life in Eagle Lake.

I first knew Mazie when she was four, maybe five, years old. This was at the Shaver home in Eagle Lake where I was studying pottery, a course taught by Mazie's mother, Louise. Mazie was a frail looking child, with the dearest smile one can imagine. She did not run as fast or yell as much as other kids, but I soon learned she was anything but "frail." Even though her voice was a bit slower than most, when she spoke others listened.

For instance, she would not hesitate to demand a "stop that!" to any playmate (even her older brother Steve) when and if teasing another or maybe even a defenseless pet animal got out of hand. No child would argue with her—they simply stopped what they were doing and went on to other games.

I began taking my young son, John, to play with Mazie while I worked in the pottery. My first impression of Mazie made me sure she would have a positive civilizing influence on John, which turned out to be true. She taught him floor games such as cards, jacks, even paper dolls, which he promptly labeled 'ol girl games' but played anyway. Mazie would just laugh at him as they became good friends and enjoyed playing together.

Later on, when they were about eight, or maybe ten years old, I was teaching dance to a group of high school girls as John and Mazie watched. Mazie came to me after the lesson and said, "Teach me to do that." I knew she meant it and we began lessons once a week.

I also took swimming. In fact, I took lessons every year and had a season pass at the swimming pool. I guess I did okay with that since I'm still around. One of the positive points about living in a small town at that age and stage in my development is that I was just a kid who was physically slow, not physically handicapped.

I remember having special times with Daddy. When I was about seven, and continuing for a number of years, Daddy would take me for a ride after supper. He would drive to the local restaurant and purchase a cigar. He always gave me the cigar ring for my finger. It was my prize. Remember "The Unsinkable Molly Brown" and her cigar ring? Along with this prize, I would get a candy bar or a piece of gum. Those trips were so very special.

Another special time with Daddy was one time he took me swimming at the local pool. He stayed to watch me swim. I remember I asked him to show me how to dive off the side of the pool. So, Daddy, as always, said okay. He leaned over the side with his arms pointed toward the bottom of the pool. You know the position. Well, I mimicked his pose and leaned into the position and dived into the pool. As I came up, I saw Daddy climbing up the ladder! He was fully clothed—billfold, hat, and all! Now, I might have been real ticked off if something like that had happened to me, but not MY DADDY. Since he was the only father at the pool, and there were all these mothers there, I'm sure he was VERY embarrassed. However, he never said a thing. We just went home.

My parents just wanted me to be like everyone else and live a full, productive, happy life. They encouraged me in each of these activities, but they were also the safety net for me when one was needed—just as any other parents would do for their child who is loved. Mother and Daddy didn't know it, but that move to the remodeled two-story house was a great help in my battle to develop my gross motor skills. Walking up and down the stairs strengthened my leg muscles as well as helped me with my balance. Sports, dancing, swimming, climbing stairs—just check out what type physical therapy is recommended now! We were ahead of our time! (Have you noticed that I write using a lot of exclamation points?) Well, I really think my life is one exclamation point after another anyway!

Carman, my other girlfriends and I loved to play paper dolls. These weren't the run-of-the-mill, store-bought, book kind. These were cut from pattern catalogs such as Butterick, McCall, and Simplicity. If a paper doll wanted to change clothes, it would most likely change hair color and posture too. Each of us had a special book in which we kept the paper dolls. Each character would have at least five to ten changes of clothes. We would have complete families, mother, father, and usually two children with a baby thrown in if we had found enough different patterns. Since my coordination was so poor I know I didn't cutout the characters, but neither Carman nor I can remember who did. (Maybe it was my fairy godmother!) Evidently, who cut them out wasn't that big of a deal. The big deal was who had the most "change of clothes" for each character.

Another thing we liked to do was play "Hell." Kids from all over the neighborhood would get together on the front porch of someone's house and play. It was sort of like a group style solitaire. If you were the person who put the king on the pile, you slapped it and yelled, "Hell!" Carman's mother put a stop to that! I guess it was too much hell and might have led to damnation as well. Anyway, we had to change the name of the game to "Pounce."

We moved from Eagle Lake when I was going into the fifth grade. It all began when Momma and I were visiting in Louisiana and Daddy was offered a promotion. But, since it entailed moving to Houston, he turned it down. When Mother and I returned from the trip, Daddy told her about his decision to not move. Mother's first words were. "Get me out of this fishbowl!"

The circumstances prompting this move were typical of what can go on in a small town. But, my mother had had enough of living "where everyone knows your face" and your business. For instance, what "friends" and community don't know for sure, they make up.

Of course it wasn't an instantaneous decision, but it was pretty darn close to it. Mother and Daddy discussed the consequences of the move—the positive and the negative. Yes, Daddy would have a promotion and pay raise. Yes, we would be out of Eagle Lake and closer to doctors and culture. But, Steve might not be the star on the football team and would most likely have to lay out a year in competition. Daddy was especially concerned about how I would adjust in a bigger school and without having the support of the friends I had all through school in Eagle Lake.

Mother, in her positive Mazie mode, said, "Mary Anna can handle anything!" And she was right. The move to Houston was the best decision my parents could have made. They had given me the home support. The school and my friends in Eagle Lake had helped give me confidence and encouraged the development of my self-esteem. I could handle anything—well, of course, I was only in the fifth grade and thought I was indomitable.

Chapter 6

Try to find the positive even through difficult situations.

Whoever said, "Sticks and stones can break my bones. But, words can never harm me" was a liar!

This section of my life has been the most difficult to write about. Words, words, words. They have started wars and caused broken hearts. They have made the strongest and most tenacious person into shy, introverts quivering and quaking like piles of Jello. And I am no exception. I didn't need anyone to tell me "it's okay." Well, folks, that just doesn't cut it.

We all know that "kids say the darndest things" and "tell it like it is;" but they also say things that are cruel and hateful. Children, who are different, whether due to race, color, creed, or physical reasons, are always told they are special and everyone should be like them. I knew I was different because of my speech and mannerism. Being different hurts. It hurts to the very core of one's being. It hurts in ways that cannot be made better with a kiss or a Band-Aid. Well, thanks be to God that I had a supportive family and was able to talk about and deal with the verbal abuse I endured.

We moved into a new area of Houston, Westbury Addition, a middle class, white-collar neighborhood. I attended Shearn Elementary School. I had to ride a school bus. It gave me the opportunity to meet most of the kids within a five-mile radius of home.

At my bus stop there was me; and then there were seven boys. All of us were within two grade levels of one another. I was teased a lot by them. Most teasing was in fun, but some was cruel. I look back on this now and I want to really believe that they did not know how cruel they could be. But, I think that this is said about all kids. I formed many friends during this time since I spent at least one and one half hours daily on the bus.

Of course, these were the same guys who would take up for me and help me at school; no-holds-barred boy friends who helped me make the transition from the small school of Eagle Lake to the large school in Houston. For the most part, these guys accepted me as one of them. Sometimes their teasing went beyond the bounds of friendship, but overall they were the ones who harassed me at the bus stop, played ball with me at home, but "Don't mess with Mazie," at school! They were right there to defend me. They gave me the spirit that is with me today.

Of course, this was the age I, sorta, kinda, woulda, liked to have been thought of as a "girlfriend" and not a girl friend. One particular friend, about whom I have fond memories, is Morrison. He lived two doors from me. We had a lot in common because our mothers were in various clubs and activities together. We played basketball in the driveways. All the guys "allowed" me to play. We also played baseball. *Looking back on this I wonder if it was because they never knew if I would hit the ball or make it to the base. I was definitely not a "given."* They became what I called "my army." Again, they accepted me as "one of the boys."

When I entered that fifth grade class, I had to stand in front of the class and tell everyone my name and from where I came. I told everyone that I had just moved from Eagle Lake to Houston during the summer. Then, I told them something that changed my life. I told the class, "My name is Mary Anna Shaver, but that my nickname is Mazie."

I was more challenged in this classroom than I had been in Eagle Lake. I had to work hard to maintain a "C" average. The competition was great and there were no exceptions made by teachers when grading my work and performance. I was just another student to the teachers.

During this year I had the mumps and chicken pox back to back. The doctors think this double whammy was a contributing factor to my speech pattern. I had always had a problem with articulation. Now my throat seemed to close up and cause more muscle damage resulting in strained, stressed speech.

At this time, my muscular tremors became more pronounced. In fact, one night at the dinner table while eating English peas, my daddy had had it with my flipping peas across the table. I can't help it if those darn things seemed to have a mind of their own and wanted to travel away from my mouth and not into it. Anyway, Daddy said he would really prefer not to have MY peas on HIS plate. He then suggested that I try holding my fork in my right hand since that hand didn't seem to shake quite as much. To my surprise, it worked.

I had never realized that one side shook more than the other. It was a big event in the Shaver family to have me keep my food contained. It didn't happen overnight of course, but hey, with determination and minor successes along the way, the peas stayed with me and no longer traveled. With this revelation (using my right hand instead of my left) daily motor skill tasks were made easier. Why hadn't the doctors suggested something like this? I feel like the astronomer who discovered the anomaly in a radio reception, "WOW!"

The following year, after struggling to try to overcome the added stressed speech difficulties, my parents made the difficult decision for me to repeat the sixth grade. They chose this year to make this difficult decision because they felt it would be less traumatic—what with my peers moving to either Pershing or Jane Long Junior High while I remained Shearon Elementary.

I was not failing in my schoolwork, but I was struggling academically as well as physically. Not only was I physically smaller than other kids my age, I was slower in many ways that count at that age, i.e. Reading, writing, running, talking, interests, and sexual maturity. We also discussed this decision with my teachers and the school counselor.

As usual, my parents did not make this decision without consulting me. I am thankful for the final decision being for me to repeat the sixth grade. It was at this time I decided I would no longer be known as "Mazie." I went back to being called Mary Anna. I had lost my "Mazie" persona and the confidence John and Carman had given me. My school peer support system had moved on and I was no longer the person known as "Mazie."

I do not remember being ridiculed very much for having to repeat the sixth grade. I was much more comfortable and happier now. Part of this comfort came from the pace (I was placed in the lowest reading group) and not having to struggle as I had the year before. Also, I was in the class with Harold, one of the boys I played with and who lived in the house behind me.

I had a protector in Harold as well as with Mrs. Mumphered, a very understanding teacher. *See, there goes that wall of protection from my SUPPORT SYSTEM—WOW!* I was happier than I had been in a long time.

I have to put in a "memorable moment" here. Mother surprised me on my birthday. She had been taking a cake decorating class. Of course one wants to share one's talents with the ones they love, right? So, she did. Boy, that is a birthday I will never forget. It was a beautiful cake. In the center of the cake was a doll with flowing hair. The cake made up the dress of the doll. You know; you've seen them. That's the okay part.

The memorable part came after the singing of "Happy Birthday." Mother nonchalantly pulled the doll from the cake in order to be able to slice the cake. An audible gasp went through the class. The doll was stark NAKED!!!!! It was a real hoot. The boys in the class were convulsed with laughter—hands over eyes and over mouths! You get the picture?

I don't remember if the cake was chocolate, strawberry or white. It could have been polka dotted for all anyone remembers, but the occasion was memorable.

The testing did not stop when I started school. In fact, when I was about twelve, I went to an ear, nose and throat specialist. (I use the term specialist with great difficulty.) In his office I sat in a chair similar to one at the dentist's. A tall man walked into the room. He had the most yellow teeth I have ever seen. He asked me to say the alphabet, looked down my throat, and then, left the room. When he came back into the room, he walked up to me, looked down at me (in more ways than one, I might add,) and said, "You talk like this because you want to. There is nothing wrong with your throat."

Mother was in the waiting room. I asked the nurse to please have my mother come in. I was very agitated, tearing up, as I told her what the doctor said. I have never before or since been so disgusted with a doctor. I told Mother, "Get me out of this place!" I was so humiliated. To think, that a professional would say such a thing, much less would say it to a child who had come to him for help. I cannot begin to find the words to convey my wrath and indignation to you, dear reader.

Later, Mother said she had never heard me speak as plain and forceful as I did then. I told her, "I'm through going to doctors for my problem, spending money for nothing. Let's just go home and deal with it." AND WE DID! From then on, the only doctor I went to was our regular family doctor, Dr. Schwartz. He understood my distress and placed me on a muscle relaxant. It was the only thing that allowed me to function as "normally" as I could. Except during pregnancy, I have been on them ever since.

That summer, before I repeated the sixth grade, I attended a Girl Scout camp along with three others from my troop. Upon arrival, I had to go through an "induction." I had to sign papers, go to the nurse, etc.

Anytime I am put under pressure, whether physical or mental, my tremors increase. Consequently, my handwriting becomes even more illegible. This in turn makes me more nervous, which makes the handwriting worse, which makes me more nervous--you know "the vicious circle." I finally finished filling out the paperwork and proceeded to the nurse. I certainly could have done without the episode that ensued.

To have my height measured I had to remove my shoes. So, I bent over to undo my shoestrings and while in this position the nurse inserted the thermometer--in my mouth. Big mistake! I was nervous, bent over, trying to untie my shoes, not fall over from lack of balance, trying to hold the thermometer in my mouth and WHAM--I bit the darn thing in half. The nurse was astonished! She became as upset as I. Anyway, she tried again.

I still had not gotten those darn shoes off and so I was back in the same position trying to untie shoestrings. I really tried to keep that thermometer in my mouth by holding it only with my lips. But, same song, second verse. I didn't bite it, but at times I breathe through my mouth. So—I dropped it. It broke again. We were finally successful in getting a temperature reading when I sat in a chair and held the "bloomin'" thing. Third time charm.

Daddy stuck around camp and put the mosquito netting up over my cot. This caused me no embarrassment although other girls did it without any help. There were other fathers still milling around.

I had a good time socially, but the physical activities were very trying. I was not accustomed to this constant physical exertion 12-18 hours a day. Scout camp pushed me past my physical limits. In swimming, I was placed in the beginner's group. Although I had been swimming recreationally since I had lived in Eagle Lake, I could not pass their "test." I could not tread water for five minutes and because of my breathing pattern I could not swim the length of the pool using the breaststroke.

At this camp I had to carry my own meal tray. This was also a first for me since all during the school year I took my lunch. Again, under pressure, especially time or being on "exhibit," I shook a lot more. Thank goodness I never spilled the contents or dropped the tray; but my food did a lot of slipping and sliding.

The weeklong camp seemed longer than seven days. I endured and came away from there, knowing that I could push my limits.

JUNIOR HIGH

When I finally made it to the 7th grade I became acquainted with a new set of friends. I attended Jane Long Junior High School. I did not participate in any after-school activities. These are the activities through which most students develop friendships. Again, I rode the bus. Every morning at 6:45 I was at the bus stop. This is when you really get to know people.

Nothing is like an early morning friendship! The same group made it back to the bus stop by 4:30pm. Ugh! I don't think I could keep those hours now. Ah! Such is youth.

I no longer had the intense struggle to keep up my grades although I still had to make a concerted effort. I "fit in" better with this group. My maturity level was more appropriate. I took ballroom dancing, which helped the progress of my social life. We would have dance parties at each other's home. I also became a part of a "clique"--the ultimate goal of teenagers. I wasn't the best dance partner the guys could have chosen, but their compassion for my condition softened any uncomfortable moments.

During this time, I had been called into Mr. Harris' office. He was the seventh grade counselor. He was trying to help me by determining whether or not I had been placed in the correct classes. He knew I had been struggling with some of my classes. He met with me and for some reason he asked me to write my autobiography. He zeroed in on the statements I made about my feeling inferior to my brother. I must add, that it was a physical inferiority, if anything. Anyway, he asked my mother to come in and discuss my situation with him.

The result of that meeting was that Mr. Harris linked Momma to Dr. Irvin A. Kraft, director of Child Study Clinics Houston Independent School District. Mother contacted him and was asked to submit an application form. She did. I am enclosing it. This is the letter that my mother wrote in response to a questionnaire. However, to the best of my knowledge, nothing became of it and it was never discussed at home—another dead end! No answers.

Houston, Texas
Jan. 12, 1959

Child study clinic

    I.   Pre-birth History
        1. Family sit. At time of preg.
            1. Immediate family situation
               Very good, married in 1934
               A Son, Steve born in 1940 Mary Anna in 1945, at this time we were living in a company house with Tidewater Oil Co. (gas recycling Div.) with whom we had been with 9 years-Mr. Shaver was shipping foremen, also was teaching a C.A.A. flying school
            2. No illness during preg. Only a very large amount of mucous discharge, which I thought was abnormal.
            3. Emotional upsets.

My mother was dying of cancer; I traveled (150mil) several times, but never alone. She died a yr. after Mary Anna's birth, I think I was emotionally normal-we had known it several years.

    4. No accidents or injuries.

II.   Delivery

    1. Water broke late afternoon, a few pains. Pains stopped, spent the night in the hospital. Then went home about 8 miles. Pains started in late afternoon about 30 minutes apart about the 3rd pain Mary Anna was born.

    2. No anesthesia was used.

    3. She did not breathe right away. I didn't see her for the first 24 hours.

III.   1. I was very happy and excited after her birth, she was exactly what I wanted, and she was awfully tiny 3 lbs. We kept a practical nurse for 30 days, not because we thought anything was wrong, she was very healthy.

    2. Bottle fed-homogenized milk

    3. a. Sitting up--4 1/2 months.

         b. Crawling-crawled in a sitting position.

         c. Walking-2 yrs.

         b. Talking-2 yrs-with a speech impediment.

         c. Toilet training: at a very early age was never a bed wetter.

IV.   General:

Our family life is a normal American family. Our standard of living I suppose is some above average and has always been. Mary Anna fits in perfect. She is not a child who wants or expects more then we can afford. She has several personal luxuries but never expresses great desire for those she doesn't have. She is very pleased to be dressed similar to her friends, not try to overdress them or visa versa. She gets along well with her friends but has never been a one or two girlfriend kind; and wants to live a close life with them. She has a very good personality, gets along swell in all walks of life, home, church, school, and socials.

Her present problem is her voice, (not the impediment) it is vocal, it seems to be a strain on her vocal cords as if she has had a severe illness and is still weak. Her whisper is perfect. She can't read aloud in school or give an illustration to the class, it isn't because she is before a group, it is the same talking to 3 and 4 yr. old children or us here in the home-it almost hurts my throat to hear her talk, she says it doesn't hurt hers. (I say she doesn't seem to have a complex about it) and yet I'm sure she does-she has a lovely smile, with lots of friendliness including what we want to try to keep.

Mary Anna's personal temperament is far above average, she is 14, has never expressed anything but normal anger, never a tantrum fit, or raised her voice at us, or made unfair demands of us. She is not jealous of any material things we other three have. Always complimentary toward us-I may add here we have always been that way toward her, she has never had a spanking in her 14 years this sounds almost untrue but she never needed it, we have never had a discipline rule she has always minded us or had a sound reason for disobedience.

Mary Anna doesn't attend church regularly, but is a highly religious little girl. She doesn't want any of us doing anything that she thinks is some what on the wrong side, I found several years ago it worried her very much-we are Methodist. We participate in social activity that we feel is in good character. Never overindulge or serve alcoholic beverages. We might be called non-drinkers, but we do on special occasions or parties. My reason for adding this is—we almost don't do it because we can tell she would rather we don't.

Mary Anna, thinks her brother Steve who is 18, is quite an idol, she also wants him to be right up to par which he is. He has never given us a worry only every day life problems. This is his first year in college he has been very successful. I might add always has been in Mary Anna's mind you might study her from this point.

Steve from 1st grade on was always popular. In his class room each year he has been voted: most popular boy, best all around boy, Duke, Master of Ceremonies, character in plays, most improved athlete, attending college on football scholarship, make 2nd team all conference 1st year.

We have never been as complimentary toward Steve as toward Mary Anna because we felt he just fell into his successes with normal participation.

Mary Anna's school life has been character in plays (a small part), May fate dancer, private dancing, baton twirling, swimming lessons, skating lessons, Brownies, Girl Scouts.

I haven't pushed her or held her back; she herself wanted them. She gave everything she had to it, worked hard, and most times was about average or a little under, but would never give up. Every one has always complimented her. She thanks them graciously, I may be wrong but think she feels a failure in her undertakings, wants so badly to feel worthy of the praise.

Mary Anna's teachers have all been so wonderful to her she has tried hard for them. I believe she is disappointed with herself.

9. Problem now facing

Is her voice physical or emotional?

1. It began in March, 1958 in the 6th grade at Shearn Elem.

2. How? I'm not sure, she had a very light case of the measles, it was so much later when I noticed her voice, I had forgotten about the measles, which didn't seem to hurt her at all.

3. What we have done since to handle it:

   a. Went to our family Dr. Harold R. Schwartz.

   b. We went for a series of examinations.

   c. He then recommended Dr. Israel H. Schuleman, Med. Tower Bldg. Whom we went to as long as he requested. I would like for you to talk with him, he seems to think her trouble is emotional but would hesitate to make the statement, without some extensive throat examinations done under anesthesia to determine the physical condition or we should give her a little more time. It wasn't any worse when school started in Sept. So far it is not any better. She has met on weekly occasions with Mr. Winston Harris, L7 Counselor or Jane Long Jr. Hi. who now has recommended you.

4.   We are mostly upset about her voice because it is affecting her school work badly, and her personally.

Thanking you
Mrs. W. N. Shaver

New schools were always opening in the area of Houston in which we lived. By the end of my seventh grade a new junior high school had opened, Johnston Junior High. This was within walking distance from my house. Thank goodness no more of those early school bus runs. During this time, I was just "one of the kids." I was even in the school choir. I performed daily with the choir, but only went on stage two times. This first time should have been my last time on stage. But, no! I had to go the second time. I felt I was an unneeded distraction during the singing and calling attention to myself because of my tremors. This was it! No more stage appearances for me. Thank goodness the year ended before any other performances were necessary.

HIGH SCHOOL

During my time in Westbury High School I had the same homeroom teacher every year with the same group of students. This certainly added stability to my high school years. These years were hard for me, especially in government and English classes as well as in my social life.

I have my home economics teacher, Mrs. Reid, to thank for helping me make it through these years. She was tough, but supportive when dealing with my problems and my feelings. I took all of the home economic classes available in my high school as my electives. Mrs. Reid was my inspiration to attend college and major in home economics. I will always remember her expression, "Don't sit there like a bump on a pickle." In other words, "move it!" I hope that everyone has the chance to experience the kind of nurturing that she gave me.

I was about sixteen when I was at one of the many of my brother's college football games. I went down to the concession stand and saw a familiar face. It was a girl I had known when I lived in Eagle Lake. I hadn't seen her in about six years. But, I thought, what the heck. I'll go say hello. I know that my speech had become more labored along with my not being able to articulate sounds as well as when I was younger, but I was not prepared for the reaction I received. She asked, "What is the matter with you? I cannot understand you."

I didn't know what to do. People were listening. I wanted to shrink. At this time in my life I didn't know why I was the way I was. I just looked at her, turned away, full of anger and disappointment. So, I found myself a private place and cried. I've never told anyone of this incident until now. I guess I didn't because I didn't want to admit I didn't know how to handle this.

I received my driver's license at the ripe old age of 17. Daddy taught me to drive using Momma's 1955 Pontiac—no power steering on this baby! I practiced driving on undeveloped roads around the area. He really put me through the paces—stopping, taking off from a stop without jerking my neck (his too!), and turning corners. Daddy and I went driving every Sunday afternoon for a year. He wanted me to be confident—in my driving and in myself. Just another way he supported me and protected me. I passed my driving tests with nooooooo problems.

During high school, I was what might be called a "Wallflower." I had opinions, but I kept them to myself. I did not want to call attention to myself because of my speech and my shakes. I didn't appreciate the glares I received from others or their rude comments like, "What did you say?" "What?" "Repeat yourself." I did not mind their asking these questions, but it was the tone and attitude that went with the questions that hurt.

As I said before, Mrs. Reid's favorite expression was, "Don't just sit there like a bump on a pickle". During my junior year I decided I was missing out on a number of things and I just had to "Move it!" I was no longer missing out on the daily school gossiping sessions. I was widening my circle of friends and letting others know that I had a distinct personality with views worth knowing and sharing. SO! I pledged to myself I would speak up when I felt like it and I would join in the laughter and to HECK with anyone's reaction.

There was an adverse side effect--I received a D in my government for one six weeks with a U in conduct. Mother went for a conference with the teacher and tried to explain why she was elated with my U. Even Momma realized I had finally come out of my self-imposed shell. She wasn't thrilled with the D for the course. I guess my government teacher thought we really belonged together because she never understood why a parent would not be upset about a U in conduct. Oh well, it takes all kinds. I became known as a chatterbox and haven't shut up since!

I am thankful that I was challenged while attending this 5A School. Although I ranked only 234 out of 306, I made it into college.

Oh, I had some very hard knocks from first grade through my senior year. My personality was changing every so often. I was confident one minute and shy the next. But, I knew if I could graduate from Westbury High School, I could make it in college.

Graduation was fun. After I had to sweat passing English. Of course, wouldn't you know, it was my last final. I was on pins and needles. Mrs. Reid was also. She could not stand the thought of my not walking across the stage with my classmates. She went to my English teacher to ask about "her" Mary Anna. She then came to see me. I didn't know what to think as she walked up to me. I wasn't really prepared for the worst, but it was in the back of my mind. She looked at me and very seriously said, " No sweat! Let's graduate!" WOW! And graduate I did!!!

I climbed many mountains during my school years. I did have support—a lot of safety nets, if you will.

Chapter 7

College is an education unto itself—a time to spread ones wings.

I had taken the ACT during my junior and senior years in high school. The scores were within the acceptance range of small colleges. I applied to Texas Woman's University (which would have put me at TWU when Carman was there, but I didn't know it at the time), North Texas State University, and Stephen F. Austin and Sam Houston State Teachers Colleges (now Sam Houston State University).

I really had my heart set on attending Sam Houston because Steve had attended. He had played his last two years of football at "Sam" and I was so proud of his achievements while there. Also, because the family attended his games, I was somewhat familiar with the campus. It was also a comfortable distance from home—about one hour and forty-five minutes.

I was elated when I received my acceptance from Sam Houston in spring of my senior year. *See, I told you it wasn't my mind that was my problem! And that was before they lowered the ACT scores to be able to enter college.*

That summer before I started college, I was riding around in Eagle Lake and saw John. He was delighted to hear that I had been accepted at Sam Houston. That was where he was going also. That was great news. We were each other's silent support system. During those four years we checked on each other and didn't hesitate to call one another if we needed anything.

I attended Sam Houston State from 1964 until 1968. It was during these years that my independent nature really kicked in. My parents would not allow me to go home every weekend and so I was on my own (which was their intention). This is the time of my life when I learned to "deal" with my shyness, my perceived handicap and remarks made by people. I learned to laugh at myself and not take myself too seriously. That is not to say everything during these years was "peachy keen" or upbeat; but I learned how to "turn a lemon into lemonade".

I learned to have a comeback to many remarks (many well intended) by friends, acquaintances, and even strangers. One such was in response to comments about my writing with my left hand, although it is the shaky side of my body. Someone would ask, "Wouldn't it be easier to write with your right hand?" I would respond, "Maybe, but it would change my personality, and I would rather not." This usually silenced everyone.

The first day was exciting as well as terrifying. Preparing to leave home for the first time had been just as exciting and shop laden for me as it had been for thousands of other students across America.

After my parents left on that first day, my nerves were really jangling. Fortunately, I was not entirely alone and therefore didn't feel totally abandoned. A high school friend, Diane, was also attending "Sam." However, she was in a different dorm and was going through her own "settling in," so I had not had a chance to see her or even communicate with her. Thank goodness I had something to look forward to. Before we left home to head to Huntsville, we had made plans to meet for supper. So, after my initial "settling in" I was feeling melancholy and a little lonely even though I was heading to Diane's. It was a big place and I was on my own for the first time in my life.

Little did I know how serendipitous that walk would be. I saw someone who looked similar to my mother. I asked myself whether or not Momma and Daddy had come back to see me or maybe just hung around to see how I would get along? I continued my walk and approached the woman. I saw that it was not Momma. As it turned out, it was Dean McDermett, the Dean of Women at Sam Houston.

She noticed my melancholy attitude and slow walk. She graciously introduced herself, asked if I was settling in all right, and told me that if I needed anything to not hesitate to call her or come by her office. Later, these words of invitation were to come back to me in my time of need.

College life was not always wonderful, nor was it a piece of cake. An example of a "not-so-wonderful" event involved the check for my tuition. It's a long story, but here goes. Daddy had opened a checking account for me at his bank. I had written my first check just before I left for college—you know, just to be sure I could and that it would clear. No problem! I was ready for college and writing checks on my own. I did not take into consideration the hassle and confusion of registration. My nerves were frayed. By the time I was to the point where I wrote my check while leaning against a wall, my handwriting was almost unrecognizable, even by me!

The check was for the largest amount I had ever written, not to say one of the few. I was certainly glad when that ordeal was over. About a week later, I received a call from the registrar's office. Now a call from the registrar's office is one of a college student's worst nightmares and I was the fortunate recipient. My check did not clear! I was aghast, humiliated, and dumbfounded.

In great distress, I immediately called Daddy; he in turn called the bank. My normal signature can be classified as almost illegible, but this signature was really, really bad. The bank was trying to protect my daddy and his money. The signatures didn't match; therefore they would not honor it. Like who would try to copy that signature?

Anyway HERE COMES MY SUPPORT SYSTEM to the rescue. Momma drove up the next day, wrote a new check, and straightened out the matter. It was suggested that I make an appointment with the Dean of Women to cover any unforeseen similar circumstances. This was like another visit to the principal's office. Momma and I went.

Dean McDermott suggested I call the speech professor, Dr. Faye Moseley, who might be able to help me during my college career. Well, gee thanks, Dean! But, did I follow her advice? Heavens no! I was 19 and didn't need to be babied. Every time I saw the Dean, and she did seem to keep cropping up in my life, she would ask me if I had made that call. Months later the Dean made the call for me since I didn't see fit to do so. This call changed my life, as you will read about later! Thank you Dean McDermott.

I had nightmares about going to the wrong class on the wrong day. I now know that this is not an unusual condition and most conscientious, first time students have the same fear. But, I actually did it!

During the first week of classes I blithely went to my English class; sat down, and got ready to take notes. Another student came up to me and wanted to know why I was in her chair. After a brief discussion I realized I had the "right string baby, but the wrong yoyo." In other words, right class, right seat, right time, WRONG DAY!

I lived in the dorm all four years while at Sam Houston. Pat was my freshman roommate, and, although she was also from Houston, I did not know her (after all, Houston is a B I G city). She had graduated from Bellaire, the rival school to Westbury. We didn't have much to say to each other that first day. She was a quiet, shy person. I thought she didn't understand me when we did speak a few sentences. Maybe she was afraid it hurt me to talk. I decided that I should explain to her about my shaky voice.

I explained to her that, although my voice was quaky and rough, it did not hurt me to talk. I couldn't explain why my voice or for that matter, my entire body, is the way it is, but I wanted to assure her that I was really okay. I was very lucky to have had her as my first roommate because she quickly accepted me.

At this point I want to write what Pat sent when I requested information for my book. I thought, "This is Pat, alright!"

I had stayed awake the night before imagining what my roommate would be like. I envisioned someone who was fat, someone who was going to borrow all my clothes, but I never had pictured you.

Mentally, I have to admit I did not know what to do. I never really knew someone with a disability such as yours or any other kind of visible disability. Emotionally, I found myself annoyed when someone would call on the phone and say something like, "Who answered the phone? What's wrong with her voice?" or I found that people would come up and ask me, "Why does Mazie talk or move like that?" I have to say it was not only other peoples' questions that were annoying, but also it was that I became annoyed with having to deal with some issues that I had never thought of before. Other than your disability, I liked you; however, I did think you could be a little pushy.

That first year, my roommate and suite mates went home each weekend. I was still shy and afraid to speak for fear of being made fun of or having to repeat myself. However, one good thing about my room, it was across from the water fountain. People congregated at the water fountain. It was a good source for new friends, good gossip, and good planning sessions for events to come. So, I just popped right out of my room and took my place with the rest of the gossips and the planning and began to establish new friendships.

On one particular weekend in October, the school was having a pajama pep rally and dance. The four girls who lived on the other side of the fountain asked me to go along with them. I had a great time. It was comforting to find out that I was not the only one to whom all of this was new. From that evening on we went places together and ate our meals together. This group soon grew to include 14 of us. We gave a lot to each other and learned a lot from each other. Even 10 years later we were still close. The bond was still there as we shared stories of our school days, our pregnancies, and our children's lives.

The second year Pat and I chose to move to different upperclassman dorms. Instead of choosing my own roommate, I allowed the dorm to place someone with me. BIG MISTAKE!

I was assigned a senior. She was a real jerk. She treated me as if my mind, not my body, was handicapped. She wanted to baby me! UGH! So, I took to spending most of my dorm time on the third floor with my REAL friends. Of course, this led to problems.

You see, back in those dark ages, we had dorm mothers and room checks. Dorm mothers were usually older women to whom we could go if we had any problems and who patrolled the halls checking for curfew violations. Wouldn't today's students have a hissy fit if that happened to them? Anyway, the mothers would go around checking to be certain all girls were in their room by 10:00 PM. They had to account for each girl.

I was never where I was supposed to be. If you weren't in your room when "Mother" checked, you were in Trouble! (Notice the capital T?) Finally the dorm mother called me to her room and questioned me as to my problem of violating the curfew rule.

I had to admit that my roommate and I did not get along very well. My roommate fussed at me for what I felt were small, insignificant incidents. She was an early bird and I was a night owl. So, about 9:00 PM every night I would go up to the third floor and hang out with my friends. The dorm mother informed me that there was a vacant room on the third floor and also that I could have a new roommate. Another girl, Davine, was unhappy living with her twin sister (go figure!). WHAM! My support system kicks in again!

Davine and I moved into the new room on the third floor. It worked so well that we roomed together for one and half years. Both of us were home economics majors, had much in common, were taking some of the same courses, and really enjoyed each other's company. After she left, I moved in with one of our suite mates.

The cafeteria was in my dorm. I ate there, three meals a day. Now, remember, I am not the most coordinated person and especially in those early days when I was unsure of myself and of my surroundings. So, of course, I spilled my tray. Can you imagine how absolutely humiliating that was? To feel like a first grader with all that collegiate aura permeating the room! No one rushed to my rescue. No one patted me on the back and said, "It's okay. We understand." So, I cleaned up the spills. After about 4 years of this I got pretty good at it! What was the alternative? Go hungry?

One day my "friends" decided to try an experiment on me. Now, they really were my friends, but I put the quotations around the word because I wonder if true friends would do this. Yes, I was a good sport about it. But, if the same experiment had been performed on any of my "normal" friends, I think that would have taken the sting out of it. Anyway, here goes.

My friends wanted to show me that my shakiness was all in my head. (Same thing the doctors had been saying for years anyway.) I was placed in our bathroom, ordered to close my eyes, had a cup placed in my left hand (the shaky hand). They filled the cup with water. The experiment was to know whether or not I shook more when there was water in the cup or when it was empty.

Well, guess what! I shook more when there was water in it. Now for some true scientific experimentation. You try it. Of course, one shakes more when there could be negative consequences such as spilling water or being laughed at when the weight of what you are holding increases. I laughed with them of course; otherwise I would have been laughed at.

Another time, I came home from a date and found my bed six feet in the air! My "friends" had placed a table under my mattress and made up my bed as I had left it. As always, they had a blast watching my face for the reaction. That's okay. Of course there was also "payback time."

One friend was forever using the term "you turd." Soooooooooooooooo one day when I was bored, I bought a candy bar (name deleted, but you know the one--nougat center, rolled in nuts and covered in chocolate). I removed the white and red wrapper from the candy bar and wrapped it in toilet paper. With a grand flourish I presented it to her and said, "It was a struggle and it took me a long time to make this gift." Oh, how I wish I had had a camera to preserve the expression on her face.

Majoring in Home Economics, I had labs in almost all courses. In the Food and Nutrition course I had to do actual cooking as well as take notes in lecture. But, that is not unusual for college students. The only difference was that I was the only one who could read my notes! Hah! At least I didn't have the problem of someone borrowing my notes and not returning them!

I also took sewing. I had a sewing machine in my dorm room. I did most of my sewing when no one was around because, just like most other things I do, I sew better when no one is watching. I was able to rest my arms on the sewing table and therefore steady my shakiness. It was hard work and took a lot of practice. (Have you tried to thread one of those needles?) But, I was determined to master this and I DID! I made dresses, suits coats along with the intricacies of putting in zippers, making bound buttonholes and flat feld seams.

One project, a fully lined suit, was the worst project I ever undertook. I thought I had accomplished this feat in plenty of time for any quick "redo" necessary. This was a dream that turned into an "all nighter" nightmare. About 6:00 the night before the due date I had completed the jacket. I held it up to feast my eyes upon my sewing glory-- a great job accomplished with a finely detailed lining. There I gazed upon my lining--seam side out! YIKES! I couldn't even blame this on any physical disability or handicap--just stupidity.

Even my roommate, Pat, remembers how hectic it was in our dorm when I was sewing:

> One of the numerous things I remember about our time at the dorm, was your sewing. I'm not sure you ever knew this, but I could never figure out how you could sew so beautifully and be so shaky. It did bother me though when you used all those pins because I was always thinking I would get up and walk around barefooted and get a pin in my foot.

Remember, at the time of the registration check fiasco, I had to go talk to the Dean of Women? She recommended that I talk to Professor Faye Moseley in speech pathology. I finally met with Dr. Moseley during my sophomore year. She is the one who diagnosed me as having cerebral palsy characteristics. Bless her! After all these years, I had a name for it and no longer had to think (in the back of my mind) that there was something I could do or could have done to overcome this impediment. She had a meeting with Momma and me and she recommended that I minor in speech pathology. Dr. Moseley offered to give me private speech therapy. I took her up on both counts—a minor in speech and therapy with her.

My reaction was, "OK, it is physical causing emotional problems—problems which were holding me back." I wanted to tell everyone I knew or with whom I had ever had any contact.

It took a while to digest this revelation in my life. I began research on cerebral palsy. I told Daddy, "I should write a book about finally being diagnosed." He said, "Alright." But I'm sure he thought, "Finish college." Daddy, being Daddy, didn't tell me, "No you can't," or "You're not capable."

This was a milestone—after a 19-year search—an answer or diagnosis was a relief. Isn't this true for anyone, not just for me? A diagnosis is easier to accept and usually one finds ways to combat a situation.

Following Dr. Moseley's advice, I took about 30 hours in speech pathology. In doing so, I learned more about myself than all the doctors had been able or willing to tell me. I thank God everyday for Dr. Moseley's help. Sometimes in class she would use me as an example. She also taught me relaxation exercises I could do for myself during class. It was so cool. She would even let me sleep in class—as long as it was due to exhaustion caused by a combination of college academic and social pressure as well as tension and nerves from coping with the tremors. "Late night" college life was definitely not an acceptable excuse.

It was during my college years that my independence got a jump-start. I know this is contrary to what Carman and John have to say, but it is when I feel I was able to separate myself from my disability and was able to be Me. I became Mazie again. My confidence returned. I had to make friends on my own and have them accept me for who and what I was, to laugh at myself if people became critical, and to turn those critical remarks into teasing with comebacks—not, sarcastic comebacks—but comebacks that turned negatives into positives.

Yes, I was hurt by many remarks made, but I couldn't let that color my life. It was at this time that I developed what I guess you would call my philosophy for my life. When I meet someone who doesn't accept my disability easily, I make a decision based on the following criteria: is it worth bothering with the person or situation? I try to make each new acquaintance comfortable with my physical condition and my speech pattern by going on with my discussion or activity or whatever I am doing as if I don't know that I am shaking or my voice is quivering.

I have found that if a person wants to get to know me, after seeing that I do not stop my activity or do not slink away they either get comfortable with me or they leave because they are the ones who are uncomfortable. That is okay with me. I accept this UNLESS it has to do with my family, with money, or I believe the cause is worth my effort.

If you are from Texas, you know about Texas A&M. Even if you are not from Texas you have probably heard about Aggies. The best jokes are Aggie jokes, sort of like "Blonde" or "Polish" jokes. Aggies are known for being the butt of jokes and for being as bright as a burned out light bulb. Whew! Talk about type casting, but you can go to the bookstore and buy books on the subject of Aggies. Here's my Aggie joke, except it wasn't a joke at the time.

During the 1960's A&M was an all male university. On weekends the Aggies would go to meet girls at either Texas Woman's University (an all-female university considered to be their "sister" school) or to Sam Houston State College.

The Aggies would arrive in droves on campus and go to the dorms. They'd start calling telephone numbers, trying to find a girl who would go out with them. I tried this route for a date a couple of times. Most of the time the results were not to my liking. I usually had a bad date.

However, I consented to go with this particular Aggie because we were going dancing. After our fourth dance, my date pulled away from me and asked, "What's wrong with you? Why are you shaky?" Darn, of course it had to be a slow dance and my quivering and quaking weren't part of the tempo. Too bad he didn't think he was the one to get me "all aquiver!"

I leaned closer and whispered in his ear, "I have CP." His reaction was hilarious or it would have been if I hadn't seen this before. He immediately asked, "Can I catch it?" Oh what wonders we do produce in our great public education system. I kept my composure and suggested we go somewhere else, where it was quiet, to get a drink so I could explain. I sometimes wonder if his foot is still in his mouth or did he scope out his intended dates any better after that? Maybe he remembers it as "a close encounter of the unknown kind."

I guess this is as good a time as any to add my "DRUNK AT 3 PM" story. This one involves my husband. Of course Jack wasn't my husband at the time. It was the first time he encountered me albeit via telephone, and like the Aggie story, it took place at Sam Houston State.

Jack was talking on the phone to his girlfriend who lived in my dorm. I walked into her room while I was talking to someone else. Jack heard me. (I never said that during my college years I was shy, quiet, and sedate.) He wanted to know who the drunk was. WELL, let me tell you, his girlfriend gave him an earful!

Most of the time I ran around with a group of friends. There was casual dating within the group, but few couples were "serious" at this time. One of the guys in the group was Elmo. Elmo and I were having a late night, all night, telephone conversation. I kept thinking about turning 21 in a week so I kept telling him I wanted to go to Trinity, Texas to buy my first beer. Huntsville was a dry town, meaning no alcoholic beverages sold in the city limits. I didn't have a car so I was hoping he would offer to take me. He spent his time on the phone trying to convince me I really didn't want to go get a beer. *Heck, I was hoping he would take me, what was he thinking I meant?* His argument was "a nice girl like you shouldn't go to a beer joint." I coyly asked him, "How do you know I am a nice girl?" He said he had been around me enough to know what kind of person I was. Oh! WOW! At last, someone who really, really liked me. But, darn it all, I wanted to "sow some wild oats!"

What did Elmo expect me to do? Sit in my room eating bonbons and reading a romantic novel? After a rather heated debate, we compromised. Finally he came to my decision. *All right, we all know that we let men talk until they think they have come up with what was our original idea in the first place!* He agreed he would go as my date and a group of us would go to the "Paper Moon" in Trinity, Texas. I finally got that drink I had been wanting. Okay, maybe it was two or three or some such number. Elmo kept buying beef jerky for me to eat so the alcohol would not be as potent when it hit my blood stream.

I had the time of my life! I danced with the dates of all my friends. This was my first one-on-one contact with Jack. And I do mean one-on-one. Fuzzy sweaters and sharp pointed tie tacs make for an interesting situation. By the end of our first dance, we were entangled. But, you will have to read the details in Jack's version of our life together. I later found out that he asked his date, Dana, about my shaking. He got an earful from her again (remember the "drunk" story?). Of course, she couldn't tell him much since I didn't even know much about my "condition." So she just said, "Mazie is Mazie."

I took the normal class load and normal courses demanded by my major. It was hard to get the Physical Education credits though. I had taken badminton, modern dance and health but I needed one other PE course. When I went to register for that semester, there was only one course open—Track and Field. The professor (that I had for modern dance) and I got a really good laugh out of this one. Both of us tried to imagine my jumping hurdles and throwing a disk. He suggested that I come back the next day and he would place me into a class more suited for me, tennis. I know you must be wondering if this was a case of "out of the frying pan, into the fire." Basically, I could have a series of two rallies but at least I wasn't falling over hurdles or dropping discuses on my feet. It gave me the last PE credit I needed. Oh well, if I couldn't laugh at situations, I would spend so much time crying.

I was very fortunate that during my years in college I did not have to work. However, during the summer of 1966 I volunteered at the United Way. I worked with children who had been diagnosed with cerebral palsy (CP). I was in charge of the afternoon program and enjoyed sing-a-longs, working puzzles, and playing games with the children. Up to this time I had never been around anyone with CP. I learned a lot from this experience.

The children were severely affected by the CP. I felt that if I did indeed have CP, which I doubted, then I was more mildly affected.

Although I had fun in college, I still cried a lot. It was hard to keep a 2.5 GPA in order to be able to stay in school. I was on probation some semesters, but never flunked out. However, I never graduated because I could not pass Government II and English IV. Well, that and another reason.

It involves my psychology professor, from whom I had taken at least two other courses. I wrote a research paper on cerebral palsy for my last psychology class. The professor called me into his office and told me he could not give me a "C" for my research report because I did site any sources for my data. I told him I had been studying about CP for the last three years and "just know" the information. He said this grade could affect my being able to graduate. I told him it really didn't matter. I was getting married in August and I couldn't see any future career for me in my chosen major of home economics or my minor in speech pathology.

My self-esteem was not helped when my psychology professor told me that I needed to reevaluate my life's plan about going to college and graduating. He told me to give him a day to think about my situation and for me to come the next day.

When I returned the next day, he had not been able to come up with a plan and told me I would never be able to do anything but operate an elevator. (I can't tell you how outraged Carman was when I told her about this. She couldn't imagine an educator, let alone a psychologist, saying such a detrimental and devastating comment to a student. I think she has a few words she would like to say to him and I don't think it has a positive adjective in it!) So, I dropped out of college lacking two courses!

Chapter 8

Love is the shortest distance between two hearts.

During college I dated two guys on a steady basis. Jack is the one who won my heart. Jack and I dated from October 1966 until August 1968. He really had time to learn how I responded in most situations. His love never faltered. To my knowledge, he never indicated to me or to any of my friends that my "handicap" was a nuisance or embarrassment or handicap to him.

Jack was an art major. He could be fun as well as serious. He liked my girl friends and seemed to fit in with "the group" I ran around with. If Jack noticed my "handicap" he never indicated it and just dealt with it. He was kind to help me when he saw I needed it and allowed me my independence when I could handle situations. I think that is one of the reasons I love him the way I do.

When Jack and I finally decided that we were really serious about each other and making a commitment we still did not rush into anything. We spent the summer of 1967 looking at rings. The looks we received along with remarks made were a real hoot. Because of my tremors we received such remarks as, "You must be awfully nervous." "Are you cold?" "Why are you shaking? It will be all right." But the best one was, "This ring looks great. It really shines because of your tremors." Jack and I left that store giggling. I'm sure the employees of that store talked for months about the very nervous couple.

I didn't know when I would receive my engagement ring or which one it would be. The big event occurred one unforgettable evening.

We had a date set for Saturday night and Jack kept calling all afternoon to check on me. I wondered what was going on and if this was going to be the night he really asked the big question. Or, was he nervous because he was getting cold feet? Our usual dates consisted of going to a show and having a Coke, or playing games at either my dorm, or if in Houston, playing games at my house.

We went to The Cellar Door. WOW! This was really splurging at such a fancy restaurant. Before we walked into the restaurant, Jack presented me with my ring. It was the one I had selected months ago. We were glowing as we walked into the restaurant. Jack proudly informed the waiter what had just occurred and what a big night this was for us.

In the fall, I saw John (my childhood playmate) on campus. I was going to the library when John came up to me. I was glad to see him but I also was thrilled to be able to show him my engagement ring. I walked to meet him with my left hand held out. He looked stunned. He held my hand as if in disbelief. In fact, he held it so long that I had to ask for my hand back. I knew that he and Marilyn had become engaged the year before so I said, " You're engaged. Don't you believe that I have found someone who wants to marry me?"

Then the brother in John took over and he asked all the brotherly questions like: Who is this guy? When did you get engaged? When are you getting married?

Jack and I spent the following year looking at pottery, china, and silver. Here our differences really came to the forefront. I would select china by price (with breakage and replacement in mind); Jack made his selection with an artist's eye as to color and style. When it came down to the nitty gritty of the final selection, Jack carried around a pretty black rimmed $20.00 a plate choice and I kept showing him the patterns costing $12.00 for a five piece place setting. We really had a hard time reaching a compromise, but compromise we did. Well, actually, I won.

To show you how much Jack really loved me and had really committed himself to living a life with me, he taught me to drive. Yes, I know Daddy had already taught me to drive, but that was using an automatic shift. Jack took on the awesome task of teaching me to drive his two-door Opel Kadette with stick shift. My first lesson was at a football stadium parking lot. This gave me plenty of room to try to become accustomed to the shifting. Talk about "jack rabbit driving". Hop, hop, hop. The look on Jack's face was priceless. I wonder if he thought I was worth it. Jack must have been a real good teacher, because after about three lessons I became a pretty good shifter!

Jack's mom (Mary), Momma, and I went looking for the perfect wedding dress. You've heard "third time charm?" Well, it was for me when it came to the selection of the perfect gown. The third one I tried on I knew was IT. All it needed was beading. Mother decided she could do the beading as well as the hemming. Bless her heart. She did a wonderful job on the beading. The hemming was another story.

Because I have a hip that is slightly higher than the other, every time I tried on the gown for hemming it would be 'hiked' up in a different place. I bet Momma hemmed and ripped and hemmed about 10 times. She was determined I would have a dress that showed a "one inch off the floor hem" all the way around.

Those days before the wedding were wild and hectic. I can close my eyes even to this day and see all the hustle and bustle. We had to take care of the usual pre-wedding chaos--getting the invitations ordered and addressed, locating a caterer, ordering flowers, and oh yes, find a place to live.

I think Mother had just as much fun as I did planning the wedding and attending wedding showers. Of course, she worried. Worried that maybe I was not ready. Worried that maybe I shouldn't have such a large wedding where I would have to walk and talk in front of so many people. My response was a definitive, "Yes! I want a church wedding. The people who are coming are family and friends. They know all about me!" But, worrying is a mother's prerogative.

Daddy was so very happy for me. He thought Jack hung the stars and the moon for having such good taste and judgment in choosing his daughter to be a part of the rest of his life.

I need to insert a comment about my getting married. Back in my early college years Momma would casually mention, "Not everyone needs to be married." She usually said this when one of my friends from back home or from college became engaged. This was a mountain that she did not want me to have to climb--a mountain of feeling rejected if I thought no one would love a person with my "handicaps."

I don't remember worrying about whether or not I would ever get married. In my naiveté I never let it color my life. I guess Momma worried about my future more than she ever wanted me to know. Not everyone has this type of situation to confront. The peak of one mountain had been scaled.

I later found out that Momma was not the only one who had this fear. My sister-in-law (Dee Dee), my brother Steve, and my daddy had this fear also. Dee Dee told me that when she and Steve were discussing their own future life together. He told her that he did not know what my future would hold. He wanted to be honest with her and let her know that he did feel a responsibility toward me. He told her that it might be possible that he would have to provide for me. With this possible added burden DeeDee said, "I do" on her wedding day. There aren't many women who would willingly go into a marriage with this type of cloud hanging over them. I might add, DeeDee met me only an hour before she said, "I do."

Three years later, Steve felt this burden lifted when I became a married woman. He knew that Jack would make me happy and that I could have a full life. Steve and I seldom talked about anything so serious and I never knew he felt this way.

I found out my daddy felt the same way. WOW! What great guys! Of course Daddy always had a special place in my heart, as did Steve, but this revelation just about burst my heart with pride and love. MY SUPPORT SYSTEM. It was ready to kick in when needed. I was sorry that Steve had gone into his marriage with this burden, but I was glad Jack was able to remove it.

The day after we mailed the wedding invitations my daddy made an interesting comment. He came up to me, put his arm around my shoulder, and said, "Just because the invitations are in the mail, you do not have to go through with this wedding." In other words, if I changed my mind, I didn't have to get married to save face. "I don't want that to be an additional pressure you have to have." OH! How I loved my daddy.

My wedding was a traditional church wedding, August 1968. We were married at St. Thomas More. I was not a Catholic, but since Jack had been raised as Catholic and my family never became involved with a church after leaving Eagle Lake I agreed to be married in Jack's church. I did go to the Pre-Caana sessions, which were pretty scary for me. I didn't know a lot of the things that the priest was referring to and just knowing that this was serious business—marriage that is—really got me thinking hard. No problem. I was ready for the commitment.

The wedding rehearsal was a more trying time for me than the wedding itself. I was not at all at ease. I was so nervous that my whole body shook. My tremors were producing a noise. I kept hearing a loud rustling sound. It was the bouquet of bows that I was carrying in place of the real thing that would be used at the wedding. The bows were shaking so hard they made noise. The priest tried to help ease my tension by saying, "Mazie, you are nervous tonight and Jack will be the nervous one tomorrow."

In the back of my mind I could hear Mother asking, "Do you really want a church wedding? Do you really want to be in front of all those people?"

Yes, darn it. It was going to be my great day with people who know and love me. I had a smidgeon of doubt but my determination prevailed.

I woke up earlier than usual on the day of the wedding. I guess that isn't an unusual happening for brides-to-be. I remember being calm and terrified at the same time. Since it had just turned light outside the house was still very quiet. I looked out on the patio and a thought came over me. I needed help getting into a new phase of my life. I felt the need of prayer. I had never felt this before. I knelt down, next to my bed, and asked God to help me with our wedding. I also asked Him to bless my family and to help me become a good wife. As I stood up from my prayer, a feeling of calmness came over me. It was a feeling I had not had during these hectic weeks. It stayed with me the entire day.

We had about 125 friends and family in the church. My roommate, Sharon, was my Maid of Honor. Nancy, another friend from college, was a bridesmaid. Jack's best man was John, a high school friend of Jack's—not my John. Rick, Jack's cousin, was the groomsman. I guess my praying paid off. I was calm, cool, and collected.

We had hired a professor of Jack's from Sam Houston to be the photographer. I had told him of my shakes, tremors, and facial grimaces. I asked him to have patience with me. I needed to be calm before he snapped any photos. The photographing of the bridal dress was taken in my parent's living room. He came face to face with what I had warned him about. It was a very long session. The proofs showed some bad posture and facial grimacing. However, we were able to select a few. He learned to photograph me by not telling me when the snap will happen. For some reason, I tend to become very tense and rigid when I know a snapshot is about to be taken. This bridal dress session was almost like a practice session. When it came to taking pictures at the wedding, he had learned my idiosyncrasies and did a great job.

My friend, Ethel, had this to say about my wedding day:

> I think the most memorable and touching moment about Mazie was the day she and Jack were married. At that time Mazie's walk was slow and stilted but that didn't bother Mazie, as she walked slowly down the aisle, a beautiful bride and Jack waiting for her with love in his eyes. My heart went out to her for her courage and I had to fight to keep the tears back.

Chapter 9

Our first place to live—together—wow! Jack's Best Man's parents had a well-kept 1930's home with an apartment upstairs. They were gracious enough to rent it to us. In addition to all the pre-wedding hectic schedule, we spent two weeks painting the apartment. Originally, the entire apartment was painted gray. We wanted a blue bedroom and a yellow kitchen with white cabinets. This was a first for me. I had never painted before. And paint I did—the walls, the cabinets, and me. But, it was GREAT!

While living in our first apartment we had no neighbors. I'm sure that in the 1930's this street had been a tree-lined, family community. Now, in 1968, it was zoned commercial. This was very depressing for me. I was used to families and activities associated with having a home. I was miserable and lonely. I passed my time cleaning house, sewing, cooking and talking on the phone to my friends.

We lived in that first apartment for 11 months. We moved to another apartment that was closer to both our parents and closer to Jack's work as a commercial artist for an advertising agency. Here I was much happier. I was back in my old "stomping grounds." I knew the area, had friends here, and best of all we had neighbors.

After paying rent for the next two years we located the perfect house and the perfect price. It was a three bedroom, one and a half bath, yellow cedar shake house. The closing on this house took longer than I believe anyone should have to spend on such a project. Do you know how many times you have to sign your name? Jack and I signed twenty-seven times. Do you know how long it takes someone, like me, to sign my entire legal name this many times? And, try to keep the signatures fairly legible? Thank goodness the realtor was my cousin, Rose Mary, who had infinite patience and understanding.

Chapter 10

Embrace the hard, trying times.
These are times of preparation for what is to come.

Because this book is being written to help establish the support system for those who need it, I will only say this about our conjugal bliss. It was as normal as anyone's. Not that I know what other people do in their bedroom, but neither Jack nor I have any complaints. After three years of being a married couple, we now wanted to become a family of three or more. So, out went the pills!

We tried for a very long three years to conceive. What about all those stories we had been told about getting pregnant on the first date?

Although I loved being married, our inability to conceive was very depressing. The act of conceiving is complicated and there are so many variables. It takes time and patience. I needed something to take my mind off conception and to help me quit worrying about it. So I decided to I branch out and to try something new. I had a friend at one of the local variety stores and I applied to work there. I was very pleased when I was hired to work in the fabric and notions department of the store. I wasn't using my college education exactly, but at least it drew upon what I had learned. I measured fabrics for customers, priced purchases and placed inventory on shelves. This was my first experience working with the public. This job only lasted for four months. I guess I was ahead of my time. The public was not ready to accept my shaking body and my labored speech. It was a mutual decision between the store manager and me that I leave. I was not a happy camper. But, I had tried! This mountain was not one I could climb! I returned to being "just a housewife."

Since I had no transportation available to me, I again became a stay-at-home wife. Mother didn't live too far from me and we did a lot of things together. I did the usual early marriage arts and crafts such as flower arranging and decoupage. Well, that and trying to get pregnant!

We had just about given up on my being able to conceive. I had appointments with a number of gynecologists. One gynecologist suspected blocked ovarian tubes and I underwent a procedure to have them unblocked. Still, no conception. I continued my quest for answers to my question, "Why can't I get pregnant?" I know many women are in a similar situation. It is difficult to explain to those who are able to conceive.

Being unhappy about not being able to get pregnant is not about not having a wonderful life with the one you love. It is just that when you do love, you want to have a child that is brought into the world as a result of this love. Family means so much to me and I thought we had so much love to give. It was a heartbreak each month when I knew this was not the month for the miracle to occur.

After many visits to many different doctors, my family physician asked me to go to one more. I really had no hopes of this doctor being any more successful determining the reason I could not conceive than any of the others.

I scheduled an appointment with Dr. Freundlich. He was glad to become my doctor and welcomed the challenge. Of course this meant more tests. What else is new? I'd been undergoing tests of one sort or another all my life. The tests revealed that one of the problems, Jack's low sperm count, was simple to correct. The other problem would just take time and have to be endured. It seemed that I ovulated only every other month. After the one problem was taken care of and the other acted upon, WHAM! I became pregnant! It was now my turn to experience the greatest joy a woman could have.

As soon as I found out I was pregnant, I stopped taking the muscle relaxant I had been taking since fifth grade. Of course, I had all sorts of doubts running through my mind. What had we done? Would I give birth to a healthy, normal child? Would my "condition" preclude a difficult delivery? Would I be able to take care of my child? Would I be a good mother? But, these are doubts and questions that each and every, caring pregnant woman has asked.

Dr. Freundlich was so good to me. He stayed close and kept watch over me. He did have to break my water, which as I understand, is not too unusual. While in the labor room everyone kept saying I was doing great.

When it came time to deliver, the doctor said he would not let me experience any pain. He said that it was possible that the pelvic muscles would tighten up and that my pelvic could break. So he decided to give me a caudal which deadened my body from the waist down. I had one labor pain and then the caudal. I can truthfully say I had labor pains or rather "A" pain. The doctor was right, or course. I probably would have broken something. It was so unnerving to me to be in pain and boy did I stiffen up on that one that I did have.

The most important event of my life was about to occur—the birth of our son, Daniel.

Chapter 11

Does God answer prayers? Yes—in His timing.
Remember, "No" is also an answer.

Then THE TIME came and it was off to the delivery room. Dr. Freundlich, himself, pushed my bed or rather walked beside me—whistling. He was whistling, "Onward Christian Soldiers." That hymn is still a favorite of mine since it marked such a momentous day in my life.

God answered my prayers. I gave birth to a healthy, normal, six pounds, nine ounces, 19 inch long baby boy, Daniel. Oh the joy of my life. I don't know who was more proud—me, Jack, Momma and Daddy, or—the doctor.

Although Momma and Daddy had three other beautiful grandchildren, they knew the special blessing we received when Daniel was born. And, the doctor—well, that's another story.

Dr. Freundlich took almost all the credit for the conception of Daniel. I would get so embarrassed when he would brag to the nurses about how long "we" worked and how proud he was of what "we" did! He will always have a special place in my heart. Thank you Dr. Freundlich.

Anyway, back to that exciting day. That evening, after the delivery, I was in the bed and it began to shake and rattle, just like a rattling cage. All the tubes I was hooked up to were banging against the bed. I kept saying, "I'm cold; I'm cold." I think I really scared my roommate. She called the nurse and told her I was really in bad shape and needed someone immediately.

As it turned out, the caudal has that effect on some people. When it wears off it makes you very nervous. With my shimmy and shakes already a part of my nervous system, you can imagine what my reaction was. Being reassured that this was normal and being given extra blankets soothed my body and my fears. Of course, when the nurses would bring in Daniel I would start the shakes all over again. But, this time, they were due to excitement and elation. Funny, Daniel never seemed to be upset with my holding him and shaking. I guess the nine months of togetherness had prepared him for life with his mother.

Momma saw me the day after I gave birth. She and I walked down the hall to the nursery. We "oohed" and "ahhed" over our bundle of joy. I was so nervous I could not stand up straight. I was standing crooked, my voice was very shaky, and the tremors had returned—with a vengeance. I guess God had given His miracle. Now I needed to go back to using the knowledge of

93

medication He had given the doctors. As soon as Daniel was born I went back on my muscle relaxers.

I did not breast feed my baby because I thought it was a little much since I was so nervous. There was no sense making myself feel guilty about not being able to provide a sufficient amount of milk when breastfeeding since nervous mothers are notorious for lack of milk.

Daniel thrived on formula. We always held him close, next to our hearts, when we fed him. In addition, this gave Jack the chance to participate. Jack was the typical father. He slept while I always got the after midnight shift.

Mother and I used to joke about this being the right day and age for me to have a baby. PAMPERS! My salvation! Or, rather Daniel's salvation. Poor kid. He just didn't know how lucky he was. He did not have to be a pincushion for my shaky attempts at fastening pins. In the 1960's I had a few cousins for whom I babysat. My aunt would prepare a diaper for me to use while she was gone. She would pin the diaper so I could just slip it on. No problem. See, there is a way around most tasks. For example, when it came time to dress Daniel, those darn little buttons always got buttoned; it just took a long time. But, since he didn't have anything with which to compare it. He thought it was "normal". Shoes had to be tied, which always was sometimes a time consuming production. I only wish Velcro had been around then.

I was a stay-at-home mom and I loved it. I read books to Daniel. I bathed and fed him just as any mother would do. I never had to play the airplane game at feeding time. Daniel never knew when I would hit the spot anyway (his mouth), so, it kept him focused on his food. The only thing I didn't do for Daniel was cut his nails or hair. Jack did these things.

I remember a time we went to Jack's family gathering. Daniel was still in the infant seat. It was time to eat. I placed Daniel in the seat and laid a few diapers across his small body. He knew what this meant. His little hands and feet began to wave and kick. My hands were shaking and jerking. Daniel began screaming because he was more than ready to eat. You know—a typical baby at feeding time.

I know that Jack's aunts were hoping I would ask one of them to feed him, but I didn't. Out of the corner of my eye I noticed that suddenly all the aunts left the room. After we had no audience, Daniel calmed down and so did I. We finished the fruit and cereal in our usual time consuming way.

I had no problem getting Daniel in and out of the car seat. Remember, in the 1970's, car seats were fairly new and not mandatory. I remember Daddy commenting on how well Daniel seemed to like riding in the car seat. He was the only one of Daddy's four grandchildren who did not fuss about being "strapped in."

Just as I thought I had the mother role down pat, up jumped another mountain. I had heard about the "baby blues' or what is now termed "postpartum depression", but I had neither. I had developed colitis. The doctor seemed to believe it was due to the stress of being pregnant and dealing with all the facets of parenting. I could not understand this! I had become the mother that I had so desperately wanted. But, it took a weeklong hospital visit and a lot of tests to convince me that my life was STRESSED! It took a special diet and a large drug bill (for about six months) to get me over this mountain. During this time I was still holding down my duties as a wife and mother.

The doctors advised us not to have any more children. The pregnancy and additional children would compound the problem of the colitis and wouldn't be conducive to helping the calming emotions I needed to handle the CP symptoms. So we put all of our time, energy, and love into being the best parents we could be for Daniel. Daniel was and is so very much worth it.

So, back to being a mother of a wonderful baby—Daniel grew and thrived in all the healthy ways. However, as I was writing this book and interviewing friends, one friend reminded me about how I worried about Daniel learning to talk. I was afraid that when he began to say words or put words into sentences he would sound like me.

Through my study in speech pathology, I knew I needed to say a lot of sounds to him. I was always doing things like saying, "La, la, la," or hiss like a snake, or just move my tongue in and out. Sure enough, he would try to mimic me. Also, when talking to him, I would try to speak slowly and enunciate very clearly. This was good for both of us.

I guess my life as a mother was like anyone else's. I didn't have anything to compare it to so I just went my merry way. Most of the time I didn't "feel" any different than any other mother. Except, one time, when Daniel was in elementary school and I was picking him up from choir practice, an incident occurred. I was sitting in the car waiting for Daniel to come out and I overheard three students talking. They were sitting on the bicycle rack right next to my car. They were saying, "Oh, that's

Daniel's mother. I don't know why, but she came up here with Daniel's dogs for "show and tell" and showed these dogs to us. She is weird. She talks funny. She walks funny. Can you believe that Daniel lets her come up to school" I couldn't believe what I was hearing. One of these children, Jeff, lived behind us. He would come over to play. I had taken him and Daniel to their children's bowling league. He knew me! Yet, he let those other children talk about me that way. And, within hearing distance of me!

SOOOOOOOO, I got out of the car, put my hands on my hips and said, "I cannot believe you all are talking the way you are. Number one, I was born like this and I cannot help it. You are sitting here talking about me loud enough that I can hear you! I think you should think about what you are doing at this moment. I pray that you don't have a child with any disability and that they are not made fun of in the way you are making fun of me and talking about me. And, Jeff, I am very disappointed in you! You know me! You come over to our house and yet, you joined in on this conversation. I feel very bad!" Then I got back into the car and waited for Daniel.

I don't remember whether or not there were any repercussions from my outburst. I hoped they would remember that when they hear or see someone that has a different way of doing things. That a person has to get through life with what God has given them. This was a sad situation.

This situation is another example of one reason I am writing *Mazie's Mountain.* I want to encourage people to stand up to being accepted for the way they are. There is no way around being the way you are. Stand up! Live life as full as any other person walking this earth! I don't deal with it very well at times. I have learned, and continue to learn, that it takes God and my support group of friends and family to help me and accept me—just as I am.

Chapter 12

Life is too short to let others spoil your dreams!

Life becomes a little blurred after all these years. I'll briefly list some of the "jobs" I've had while living in Alief. Of course, most were "freebies" in other words—no pay. This does not mean that I took my responsibilities lightly. Before Daniel was born I made most of my clothes. After all, I majored in Home Economics in college even if I didn't receive a degree. After Daniel arrived, I spent a lot of time learning to parent and being involved with neighbors who had the same interests—home and children. My activities included bowling on a bowling league, playing bridge, and participating in many church and school activities. One might say I kept very busy.

Daddy Pete, my father-in-law, had this to say about the way I handled my everyday life. "Nothing is easy for her but she just hangs in there. I have always admired her for her independence—even though she might be having trouble doing something—she wanted no help."

I enjoyed doing volunteer work at Twice Blessed, a resale shop, supported by my church. When we moved to Alief, I joined the Huntington Village Garden Club. And therein lies a tale!

I joined the club because I wanted to be involved in something in order to be Mazie, not Daniel's mother or Jack's wife. The club met in the evenings so Jack was able to be with Daniel. This was important to me—I'd have time off and Daniel and Jack could have quality time together.

The president of the garden club, at the time I began attending, was not really thrilled with my being there. My perception was that she wanted me to go home, never to return. I went home and told Jack my impression of my reception by the president. I also told him that, although I am a fairly intelligent woman, I was going to have to prove my worth!!!!!

Soooooo, when time for the next meeting rolled around, there I was—right in her face. If there was a job the club needed to be done, I volunteered. The president would pretend I did not speak until others brought it to her attention. Then, lo and behold, she said how sincerely sorry she was that she had not heard me. If you believe that I have some ocean front property in Arizona!

It was not long until I was placed on a committee. I was on many during the first several years. I headed up the craft section for the club. I became Vice-president, meaning I was the program

101

chairman. Yes, back then it was still politically correct to say, "chairman."

This was definitely a challenge. It was my responsibility to find speakers, put the yearbook together and call each member in order to keep our meetings running smoothly. In 1978, our home was on the Christmas Home Tour. Jack became very involved and now the shoe was on the other foot, as he became known as "Mazie's husband." He had to paint and make minor repairs inside and outside our home. It was great!

The members of the garden club spent an entire year getting ready for this tour. We were divided into groups assigned to specific homes that would be on the tour. We worked together once a week in order to make decorations for EACH room in each home. WOW! We had a blast and really got to know each other in unique ways.

No one had any secrets or skeletons in the closet any more by the end of that year. The next year I became President of the Huntington Village Garden Club and literally wore out everyone. I knew how to delegate—and that I did!

Chapter 13

Live in harmony with one another:
We do not know how long we have on this earth.

The Open House and Christmas were the last time there
would be that much joy in my home for quite a while. February
17, 1979 my greatest supporter, my Daddy, died. Daddy's death
was hard for Momma, Steve, DeeDee, Jack, myself and his four
grandchildren. I will explain why. . .

Momma and Daddy had purchased a vacation home on Lake
Livingston. They bought this with all of us in mind. Not
knowing, how well it would mesh us, as a family. It had three
bedrooms, two baths and plenty of room. It slept ten or more.
Steve's family and my family joined Momma and Daddy many
times throughout the years.

They began spending most weekends at the lake. Because,
they liked going to fish or being out of the big city of Houston.
For the first few months they didn't have a telephone. Since I
was pregnant when they first purchased the lake house, this
made them nervous. So, Daddy arranged a deal with one of the
lake's marinas across from them.

He informed them that his daughter was due to have his fourth grandchild in the next coming months. He asked if I could call the marina if it became necessary for me to get in touch with him and Momma, and would they deliver the message across the lake. My parents always used every precaution they knew. This plan eased their minds. As it turned out, I didn't have to use the plan.

All of the family enjoyed the lake house, especially the four grandchildren. There was so much to do: fishing, swimming, hiking and yes…boat riding. Momma and Daddy named the lake house, "The Shaver Haven."

Momma and Daddy taught the grandchildren how to bait a hook and catch a fish. Each grandchild got to stay at least a week with MeeMaw and PawPaw (as they called them).

MeeMaw's favorite thing was letting them help or watch while she cooked. She had more time and patience than DeeDee and I. She also liked to watch for "Charlie," the alligator. Almost every night after dark "Charlie" came up the slough, from a swamp, not far from the pier. There would be MeeMaw and her grandkids holding the flashlight while watching for two slow moving red eyes. That was "Charlie."

PawPaw loved to just watch and be around his grandchildren. He could really tell stories. His grandchildren were like his shadow. They followed him everywhere and asked many questions. On long walks while at the lake, he showed them where "Charlie" must have lived—where "Charlie's" footprints crossed the road. He asked them to never come on this path by themselves. They always listened to PawPaw!

He also taught them to drive his boat. PawPaw would go boat riding several times a day. Daniel would tell me that he drove the boat in "B's" and "D's". This meant he drove it so the boat would make those shapes in the wave on the water.

Another nightly event, only after dressed for bed, was a cup of melorine—not in a bowl, but a coffee cup with a spoon, with only, one and a half scoops. For some reason, there was never any fussing, about the amount—one and a half scoops and that was it!

Holidays, vacations and weekends were spent at the lake more than our homes. It was so relaxing for all of us. I want to tell you an example of "Christmas as Shaver's Haven."

Christmas Eve started with a rather light and easy supper. We exchanged gifts, but only after the kitchen was spotless. It was an unusual sight—MeeMaw always had a lot of helpers on this special evening. The kitchen was full of "hustle and bustle" and anticipation. The four grandchildren could not work fast enough. The opening of the gifts lasted for hours. We opened one at a time. Then off to bed to wait for Santa!

Since the house didn't have a chimney, we told the kids that Santa crossed the lake and came down the vent that was over the oven. After a few hours, Steve would go outside and rattle his keys. The keys sounded like sleigh bells. After this—not a creature would stir, not even a child. Finally it would be Christmas morning. Santa had come! The day would be filled with a lot of Love, Joy, and Food!

After Daddy retired from working for Getty Oil, he and Momma had made their home in Livingston, Texas. Even though they had the lake house. They bought a home in town. So, the road from their home to the lake, were minutes apart.

Momma and Daddy only enjoyed this retirement life together in Livingston for about 15 months before Daddy developed prostate trouble. He went into Houston for surgery and was in the hospital for about five days. We thought he was doing well, well enough to leave the hospital. He was to come to our house to convalesce for a few days before returning home. That Saturday, Jack went in to the hospital to take Momma for a visit with Daddy. Daniel and I stayed home to get Daniel's room ready for "PawPaw", as Daniel called him. Daddy never made it. He died that afternoon from a heart attack.

As for most people when there is a death in the family, the weekend was busy with friends and family coming and going. Daniel did not understand what was happening, even though we told him that his "PawPaw" died. At his age, he did not have our understanding of death. Not only did his "PawPaw" not come home, his momma was crying all the time, and his "MeeMaw" was not the fun "MeeMaw" he was used to. I was in shock. I could not believe this was happening to me. Daddy was my "god on earth." In my mind he could make my life's trials easier. He pulled me up whenever I could not get up, whether physically or emotionally. He was my rock. Now my rock was crushed. Gone. Even though I had been married for ten years, Jack was not my daddy.

Also, Daniel's fifth birthday was coming up on Monday and all these people were around, yet, no one was bringing him a birthday present. Bless his heart; he was really confused.

Mother wanted to have Daddy's funeral on the Monday following his death. I just could not bear that. That was the birthday of my son. God must have heard my prayers because

107

the funeral home could not schedule the funeral until Tuesday. It was hard! God answered my prayer! Even though it was what I wanted, I was still in shock.

On the Monday following Daddy's death, instead of having a funeral, we had cake. Jack took over the birthday cake making. He made the traditional carrot cake and really did a great job decorating it. He impressed all the friends and relatives who were still dropping by. They didn't know that I was usually the baker and Jack the decorator!

The hardest part of the very long weekend was that Mother asked me not to cry. Can you believe that? I have no idea why she would ask that of me. Thank goodness I had a neighbor with whom I was very close. I would go next door and seek refuge as well as a place to cry. They understood!

Momma stayed with me until Friday. Daniel and I took her home to Livingston where Steve, DeeDee and their three children met us. We wanted to help ease Momma's pain during that vulnerable time.

Steve and I started sorting many of Daddy's things. It was hard to believe that Daddy would no longer be here, no longer look at or touch his belongings. As hard as this was to do, both of us had to be strong for Momma. While cleaning out one set of chest of drawers, we found the scrapbook about Steve the scrapbook I referred to at the beginning of this book.

The next difficult step all of us had to take was to go to the lake house. Here there were many great memories of Daddy—out in the boat on Lake Livingston, fishing off the pier, cleaning fish. As I said, Daddy had named the lake house "The Shaver Haven." Now, it would never be the haven for me that it had been when my daddy was alive. It must have not been the safe haven for Momma either. About a year after Daddy's death she sold it.

Steve and his family stayed for the weekend and Daniel and I stayed for about a week. The really big adjustment for Momma would come after everyone left and she would have to cope on her own.

After the hustle and bustle of Steve and his family leaving, I had more time to reflect upon the death of that great man, my daddy. I had lost so much when he died. I began to grieve anew. This grief lasted for about six years.

Remember the colitis I had after Daniel was born? Well it returned—about six months after Daddy's death. The doctor explained to me I would need to live a life with no stress. He knew that was simply not happening and would be near impossible to achieve. I needed to eat properly and take care of my nerves. At least I knew what it was and how to treat it. With time and medicine, I slowly got the colitis under control. Jack was so worried. He tried to make my life less stressful.

The whole Shaver family was broken for quite a while. We helped each other get over the first birthdays and holidays. It was not easy. Life was different for each of us.

Chapter 14

Do not ask why? Ask how?

While living in Alief, Texas, we belonged to the Canterbury United Methodist Church. I was very involved in the United Methodist Women (UMW) and held various positions including vice-president. Different people had different reactions to me. Some would smile and walk on by. Some would turn their head or turn around in order to avoid me. And then, some became my dearest friends. When I asked one of my best friends, Linda Linn, from Canterbury to write something about her first impressions when she met me, she sent the following:

> I was a member of the Seekers Sunday School Class, which was a part of Canterbury United Methodist Church in Houston, Texas, in 1980 when Jack and Mazie became members of that class. At that time I did no know what was "wrong" with Mazie. ....whether it was a temporary or a permanent thing. At first I thought she might be recovering from a stroke....she had difficulty speaking and she shook a lot. My experience with "handicapped" (there's that "H" word) people prior to meeting her had been limited to people with temporary handicaps such as broken bones or surgeries. At that time I had never had close contact with anyone who

had a condition that wasn't going to improve. Mazie was a first for me and I didn't quite know how to deal with her.

The Seekers Class had a shared leadership which meant that anyone could teach a lesson if they so desired….no experience was necessary. One Sunday we were trying to get volunteers lined up to teach in the weeks to come and Mazie was asked if she would like to take a Sunday. Mazie commented that the only subject she knew anything about was C.P. We all said, "Fine! Talk about that."—and, she did. She got up in front of all of us and told us what her life had been like and she told it with humor and not a trace of self-pity. I learned that day exactly how to treat Mazie…just like everyone else!

While at Canterbury, I also presented programs, was in charge of supplies for our summer Vacation Bible School, and for two years coordinated the craft bazaar. The bazaar was another one of those yearlong projects, although I did it for two years. I was in charge of everything from purchasing supplies, making crafts, and advertising. You name it! It was a great experience. Of course, I couldn't have done it without my great support system.

I would come up with the ideas for items to be made to sell at the bazaar. After getting approval from the members of the bazaar group, I would search the town for the necessary supplies. After obtaining the supplies, the "crafty" ladies of the church would do the sewing, gluing, and painting. I don't know if it is my great knack for getting people to do what is needed to be done or if they just do it to get me to leave them alone. Whatever, I do get the job done. Notice that no matter what I undertake, I am almost always successful; my support system follows me!

I also began taking ceramic classes. Yes, ceramics!—the art of making things from pottery. I didn't always start by pouring the slip, but I took the greenware to the finished ceramics. I used various techniques including hand painting, under/over glazing, air brushing, and gold application. The size of the pieces ranged from intricate Christmas ornaments to three-foot statues. Carman still has the swan that I finished for her. I can't believe the neck hasn't been broken.

Of course I broke things! Breaking usually happened when I was cleaning the greenware. So, take one down, sweep it up and begin again! It wasn't worth crying over. As a matter of fact, my nativity sets were notorious for their durability. After all, with all those fingers, donkey ears, etc. glued back on with "patch attach" they were pretty sturdy! I should have bought stock in that company!

Jack decided that I was spending too much money at the ceramic shop. We were on a strict budget. He said I would have to stop with the ceramic classes and buying pottery and paints.

The day after we had this discussion, I went to the little shop where I was doing all my ceramics. I explained that this was my "swan song" so to speak.

Again, the SUPPORT SYSTEM came to my rescue. I was offered a job—work for greenware and supplies. Now I could still work with ceramics and not have to pay for it. Great! Picture this—someone with the shakes and shimmies working in a ceramic shop, moving, pricing, and selling greenware—a bull in a china shop?

Here's a comment by Pat, a bridge-playing friend, about my dexterity:

> I was amazed at her ability do so many things which required such fine motor skills and finger dexterity, due to her unsteadiness. She was always involved in a project or cause of some kind and would devote time and effort to get the job done.

In addition to working with ceramics, I have been a member of several bridge clubs, a women's bowling league (averaging 100 to 150). When Daniel was in kindergarten, I helped out with the art center projects once a week, as did many other mothers. I was an Assistant Cub Master when Daniel was in Cub Scouts. These are just a few of the activities that kept me busy.

I can't leave this part of my life without telling a couple of stories about my interaction with friends. Jack and I would go to parties and of course alcohol was served. Since I wasn't on a daily dose of tranquilizers I would imbibe at these parties. After about five drinks my friends knew I had had enough—I would start holding my drinks in my left hand and lo and behold—no tremors! I seldom did this so don't get bent out of shape and think that I was in danger of becoming an alcoholic. This might have happened about once or twice a year.

Then there was one evening at one of our bridge clubs. This guy was the player who was playing to my left; in other words, he would play after I laid my card on the table. I tend to finger the cards as I am thinking. I hold my cards in my shaky left hand and play with my right hand—the one that doesn't shake quite so much. I was thinking about which card to play. He was watching me finger my cards. He predetermined which card I would be playing and thought I had played a different card than the one I had put on the table. When he played his card, he played the wrong one. This led to my winning the hand. He blamed me for his mistake. He said, "Mazie, you and your shakes!" I replied, "Wrong. I used my good hand and you just thought I was going to play the one I was fingering. You had better watch all of my fingering." So, from then on, everyone teased me about my "fingering."

Picture
OF THE WEEK

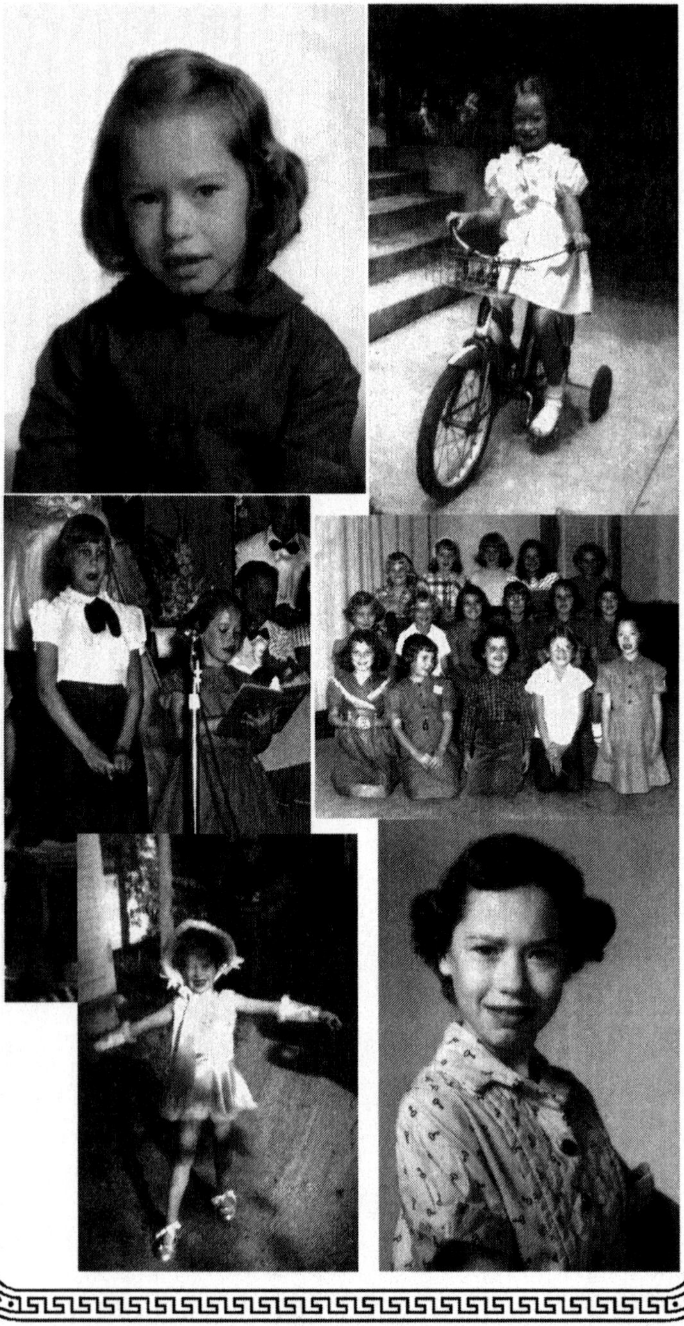

Chapter 15

Rise above it—adversity!

In 1987, we moved about 30 miles "down the road" to the outskirts of Sealy, Texas. Daniel was in the eighth grade and I wanted to be active in everything. My life became as active as it had ever been. I was active in church as the youth director and as vice-president of the United Methodist Women. I did not let my "disability" slow me down or stop me from being "out front and in your face," "take charge" type of woman. In fact, my friend Becky has this to say about me:

> Several years ago, I was teaching Vacation Bible School along with Mazie. At the end of the week, we had a little program for the parents. The Sunday before, Mazie made an announcement during church of the upcoming event. As she stood before the congregation, I began to feel empathy for her but then I stopped and took a good look at her. She was not embarrassed and even though I knew it must be hard for her, she continued. I thought to myself "Why didn't someone else do the announcement?" Then I asked myself why would I think that. She obviously had never let her disease dictate her choices. Even though it would have been easier for her to let someone else make the announcement, she didn't choose to. She was not embarrassed and so since she was not, no one was embarrassed for her.

When Daniel went into high school my life became even more hectic. I was involved with his scout troop (Jack was also very active.) I was active in the band boosters and became vice president. This honor was not given me until the third year of my participation.

The first year I ran for reporter but no one voted for me. I spent that first year after my defeat voicing my concerns, my ideas, and acting upon these ideas. I took charge or delegated, as each task was assigned to me. The person who was elected president, later told me if the boosters had know how valuable I would be to them I would have been elected in a heartbeat!

Daniel became interested in the theater and the arts—so, of course, I did too! He had a beautiful speaking voice. I encouraged him to take speech in high school. I felt that this was good reinforcement and that every person needs to be able to stand up in front of a group and be able to speak without being hesitant or nervous. As it turned out, he took Speech his freshman year and fell in love with it. That begins another chapter in my life.

I became involved in preparing costumes for Daniel's drama class and drama club. In fact, after seeing my work for their production of "Lil Abner," the drama teacher decided I would be good at making and locating costumes. Costume making certainly had its humorous moments. You can understand this better by reading this comment made by Daniel's drama teacher, Jean Adams.

One particularly event involving Mazie sticks out in my mind. We were doing the musical "Bye Bye Birdie" and she volunteered to help make the costumes. I knew that she could sew, although I had never seen her in action. We needed about twenty double-sided circular skirts. I remember Mazie sprawled out on our theatre floor with hundreds of yards of fabric, cutting out patterns. No big deal, huh? If you've ever seen scary and pretty funny all rolled into one. I was so fascinated that she could actually cut all those skirts out, never mind sew them. But, she did. She had figured out that if she used a pair of electric scissors she could control the situation a whole lot better. My lesson from this experience: You are only as limited as your attitude. Once again, her lesson for my life wins out.

Chapter 16

Give and you will receive.
We who give are the blest.

About this time in my life I acquired another son, Tracie. The great thing about this was no nine months waiting and no wondering what sex, weight, length or checking out the fingers and toes. Guess I have to tell you a little about this addition. His mother had passed away from cancer when he was about nine or ten. His father had moved from Sealy and had had little or no contact with him. Tracie had been living with his sister for the past five years, but she and her family were moving from Sealy. Tracie wanted to finish high school in Sealy. Members of our church who knew his situation and knew that we had a close and secure family suggested that we might want to help out. Helping out meant having Tracie move into our home and become part of our family.

None of us responded immediately—Jack, Daniel, or me. This was something that could not be undertaken lightly. We decided to have a family meeting. After all, Daniel would need to have a say in this as much as we did. We discussed the pros and cons for us as well as for Tracie. Tracie won, hands down.

After the family conference, Daniel went to town and brought Tracie out to the house. Poor Tracie. He had never even been to our home before and here he was, put into the position of making such a decision.

We agreed that we would all try it until school was out for the year, which was about six months. As they say, "a funny thing happened on the way to the forum." We never did have that six-month meeting. He became such an integrated part of our family that the questions we thought might arise never did.

Tracie lived with us for three years. Our only goal for Tracie was that he graduate from high school. This goal was achieved. He was the first of his family in three generations to graduate from high school. Just as we had done for Daniel the year before, we gave Tracie a large graduation party. His sister invited their entire family. It made him feel so good about himself. After his graduation, he enlisted in the Marines. Not just any branch of the armed service, he had to be "one of the few, the proud, the brave." He became a sergeant in the Military Police. I guess after the life he had led, the Marines gave him the security and family belonging that we hope we started for him. I am so proud of him.

Carman e-mailed Tracie and asked him to comment on life with the Petree's. Here is his e-mail

Let's see, where do I start. I came to live with Mazie some time in 1991 I believe. I was in my junior year in high school and needed a place to live. To go back a bit further, my mother passed away when I very young and I moved in with my sister and her husband. They decided to divorce and my sister moved to the next town over, Columbus [Texas]. I wasn't about to move to a new town that close to graduation. I had talked to some of my friends who were also friends of Mazie. I guess word had gotten to Mazie one way or the other and one night I got a phone call. It was Mazie and she was sending Daniel to pick me up.

I didn't know Mazie very well. Her son and I were in a few of the same classes and were pretty good friends. But really I only knew Mazie very vaguely. I can remember be taken aback a bit by Mazie's condition. I really didn't know what to think as I guess many people would. However, it didn't take me very long to figure out that her heart was definitely in the right place.

Anyway, Daniel came to pick me up and we drove out to his house. When I got there Mazie was very happy to see me and we talked for a while. Finally, she told me that she knew of my situation and said she might have a solution. They had a spare bedroom that was not being used and that I was more than welcome to live with them if I wanted to. She didn't make me decide right away though and told me to go home and think about it. It sure didn't take me very long to decide because I was calling them the next night asking when I could move in.

In the two years that I lived with Mazie it was probably the closest thing to a "classic" family that I had ever had. Living with Mazie had given me the stability that I needed to finish high school and succeed at whatever I wanted to do. Mazie never forced Dan and I to be "brothers" because she knew we were both very different people. However, she treated me like her own son. I had a job and was always working but I can remember being helped out with gas money or lunch money...or even the occasional pair of jeans when I needed it. Family trips to various places were always fun and Mazie always made sure about that. Mazie was truly the best "mother" I could have had short of my own. I think my Mom would have been very pleased with the way she raised me for the short time that I did live there. Those two years have made a forever lasting impression on me that I am likely to never forget.

She helped me get through two girlfriends, an ex-wife, my first car, helped pick out my first suit, made me do my homework, saw to it that I ate regularly, make it to work on time, and saw me off to boot camp the morning that I left. I can still remember how I was back then too. It couldn't have been easy for her. Daniel was the type to stay at home all the time and rarely went out. I, on the other hand, was always out with my friends to the very limits of my curfew, staying the night at my girlfriend's house, and had the occasional underage beer. All of which, unbeknownst to me, she seemed to know all about it without me having ever said a word. I always wondered how she knew. A mother's intuition I guess. But like I said, it couldn't have been easy for her dealing with all of these problems. But all in all, I think she did an excellent job of raising a rowdy teenager.

Mazie truly is a special woman. There really isn't any other way to describe her. To say anything less would definitely be an injustice to her.

Chapter 17

Take time to smile or just to listen to others.

In 1990 I began another addition to my life. I guess I felt I
didn't have enough to do!!! I started volunteering one day a week
in the artisan program of Willow River Farm. Willow River Farm
is a community living facility for the mentally challenged adults.

The first mandate of Willow River Farm is for it to be an
answer for loved ones to have a home even after the parents have
passed away. There are nine cottages with a maximum of nine
residents in each cottage. Each cottage has its own family style
living arrangements. The residents range in chronological age from
20 years to 60 years, but mentally and emotionally from nine
years of age.

One day, while I was at The Farm, assisting a couple of the
residents make baskets, a tour arrived from Sam Houston State.
My past was haunting me. Who was in charge of the tour but my
former psychology professor, the ONE I talked about earlier in
this book! I just kept working, hoping he would pass on by.

However, he saw me and came up to me. He said he never
forgets a face, but couldn't remember names. He asked if I had

attended Sam Houston. I introduced myself and I told him that I had taken psychology under him while attending Sam Houston. We had a brief conversation, but I never brought up our conversation that had so devastated me. I did make certain that he knew I had married, lived close by and was doing volunteer work-just in case he had any misperceptions as to my being there.

In 1991, I became employed as a residential relief counselor. As a counselor I had to be very versatile. The job entailed more that just being a warm body in the house and cooking the meals. I had to undergo training expected of all employees. This training was two phases— medical and non-medical. Medically, I had to be trained in first aid, CPR, and self-medication (overseeing residents take their prescriptions). Non-medical included van training and preventable management of aggressive behavior or PMAB.

I was also expected to oversee the learning of life skills. These skills included teaching the residents about setting the table, cleaning off the table after meals, preparing various phases of the meal, keeping their rooms, washing their clothes, budgeting for their outings and shopping needs and taking them on outings. These outings were not just an "around the block" type outings. I drove them to Houston and Sealy to shopping malls, to attend picture shows, to attend church, and even to Galveston. Here we went to a special Mardi Gras party.

Another time, a coworker and I took a van with eight residents for a week in San Antonio. We stayed in a hotel; visited the Alamo and the zoo. We even loaded up the residents and drove to Austin where we toured the Capitol. On the way back to San Antonio from Austin, we stopped and shopped. There is a great mall between the two cities. But, taking eight women shopping is a definite CHORE. They had to stay together, but each had different interests and different stores they wanted to go into. It was like herding geese—a lot of squawking, many ruffled feather; but mission accomplished.

After returning to San Antonio, we went on a downtown walk. The frustration of keeping all together was compounded when one resident, who couldn't walk as fast as everyone else, just gave up and sat down. She sat there for about thirty minutes while everyone urged her to get up and get moving. Finally, she got up and walked for a little way and then sat down again. Off and on this took about three hours.

The last time she decided to sit down it was at a busy corner. Some good Samaritans saw our dilemma, and came to our rescue. I flagged down a cab and they assisted me in getting the resident into it. This was a good example of what was required for this job. It required skills, patience, and the ability to think one or two steps ahead of the needs and thoughts of the residents.

I worked on as "as needed" basis. In other words, I was a substitute for a cottage counselor when they were out due to illness, vacation, or "no show." I usually put in about 20 hours per week. This working arrangement was great. I always had the opportunity to decline in the event I had other plans. Also, because I usually went to work when called, the employees liked to stay on my good side so I wouldn't hesitate to work for them.

My supervisor at the Farm told me this story. She said that when she first met me she thought to herself, "Why is she working here? Maybe she lives here and isn't working here. Maybe she is one of the residents." Then, she saw me drive off with a vanload of residents. Then she realized I was not a resident; I worked there.

She's not the only one who thinks this. Here's another example. Once a year Willow Farm has a fund-raiser called "Novemberfest." Through this, they are able to make thousands of dollars in one day. I attended one year, but have not been back since. I can always come up with some sort of excuse. I love helping prepare for it, but will not attend this event.

The year I did attend left a lasting impression on me. It was very embarrassing for me and for the residents. The people who came thought I lived there, and not as a counselor. When I would talk to the visitors I could tell by their actions, or should I say reactions, to my conversation that they were thinking, "She's got her disabilities and she is working with these people? Why is that?"

Well, I think that the person who hired me could see that I could be a role model for the residents. I can show them that I have accepted the way I am and they can also. I think this may be one of the assets I give the residents. They can go on with their life and live it to the fullest.

Over the years I have gained the trust of most of the residents. They respect my suggestions and frequently come to me for advice. They usually felt better after we talked over whatever was bothering them. When they felt better about the situation or themselves then I would feel good. Working with the population of Willow River Farm community has the reward of being a part in bettering the lives of these individuals and most importantly, the love I receive in turn. Sometimes, all I need to give is my time. Time spent in getting a resident to smile when they are frustrated, helping them accomplish a simple task, or taking the time to listen is all that is needed.

My friend, Joanne, understands why I am so blessed to work at Willow River. She wrote, "I feel God was working with her and led her to her new job at Willow River. She has so much love and understanding for all of her friends out there."

Chapter 18

Never give up on your dream.

In 1994, I fulfilled a life-long dream. I opened my own shop.
Me! Mazie! Of course it was a family and friend effort. WHAM!
Here comes my support system. My sign "MAZIE'S"—out
front and in your face. Not bad for someone who would only be
able to "operate an elevator"! I owned and "operated" my own
gift shop.

At the top of my support system were Jack and Daniel.
They had the dubious honor of doing the manual work—making
the sign, putting it up, moving in fixtures and arranging them.
Since both of them are artistic, their input was invaluable. They
also had to "put up" with my highs and lows as I would be
ecstatic one minute and filled with doubt and trepidation the next.

One always needs financial support and my support system
kicked in again when two of my friends, who believed in me and
in my new venture or I guess I should say adventure, asked to
contribute funds (both want to remain anonymous). I also
received support from other businesses in Sealy. In some ways,
businesses are one big family. Without the support of my

clientele, MAZIE'S would never have had the opportunity to succeed.

MAZIE'S was located in downtown Sealy, in a turn of the century building. My landlord had restored the building to its the original look. I joined the Chamber of Commerce. MAZIE'S had two ribbon cuttings or openings. The first had one of the largest turnouts for the opening of a new store. Since this grand opening went over so well, when I expanded and added antiques, the Chamber had a second grand opening for me.

MAZIE'S began as a gift and craft shop. I had always wanted to have a gift shop with only hand-made items. Because I was so "crafty" I had accumulated a number of items that I thought would sell. I also had people bring in items on consignment. I knew many talented people in Sealy through my community involvement. I had sufficient inventory to fill the front of the large building I was leasing. I was thrilled.

After a year, I went to "Dallas Market" (now that's an experience), something I would never have dreamed I'd be doing. I discovered that at Market no one cares about your physical attributes, just your money. Decisions, decisions, decisions; that best describes Market. You've heard the song about miles and miles of Texas? Well, there were miles and miles of merchandise.

132

I had to be very selective since I was on a budget. I have to tell you that one of my decisions created a monster—the "name necklaces."

I bought alphabetized pewter letters, put them on a string and spelled out names. Now, that was something to watch. Ol' shaky Mazie making necklaces by lacing letters together. Patience, Patience, Patience!!! I gave two necklaces to friends. That's all it took. Before I knew it, every high school student wanted one. Then, it filtered down to the junior high and elementary, pre-school and relatives of all these students. I tied each knot and slipknot for each necklace. Most necklaces were made while the customer waited. I averaged selling about 100 letters per week. I was making about 10 a day for about one and a half years. At one time I had about 30 or 40 ready to be completed while I ordered more letters! WOW! Carman had one made and took it back to Del Rio. I had to make some for Carman's employees and ship them to her.

I appreciate the fact that the fad caught on in Sealy. Of course, all things must come to an end and so did this fad. That's when I decided to expand the business and add antiques. This addition not only expanded my inventory, it expanded my business network and knowledge about antiques. I wasn't certain handmade gifts and antiques would mix. I was wrong. They really complimented each other.

I wish I could say that MAZIE'S was a rip-roaring success. But, as anyone in business knows, you have your good days and your bad days. There were some days that were so boring. I once remarked to Jack that when I walked down the streets of Sealy all kinds of people waved at me. Of course, being the outgoing person I am, I waved back. Some would even strike up a conversation with me. You know, the usual, "How are you?" "How are things going?" I would reply to their questions. However, I had no idea who some of the people were. Jack told me that everyone knew who I was because my name is spelled out above the door for the entire world to see. He had a valid point.

I have great and not so great memories of MAZIE'S. I have to tell one tale that out-shines all others.

One boring day (thank goodness I was alone, I think) a middle-aged man walked into the shop. He was holding up his pants, pulling and tugging them while saying, "I put on the wrong pants today." I was standing right beside him showing him a Christmas item. All of a sudden he let his pants fall to the floor. With much aplomb, I turned to him and said, "You lost your pants." He apologized. I immediately walked away and said, "You'd better go home and change." He turned to go out the door and glanced back at me. I said, "You shocked me!" His reply—"Was it a pleasurable shock?" I hollered, "NO! GET OUT!" He left. I never saw him again. I later heard he was "pulling" the same stunt at two other stores in Sealy and then at stores in Bellville, north of Sealy.

After this "quaint" visitor left, I called my friend Jackie who had a shop around the corner. We had established a code that if one of us called the other and said, "You have a package here" it meant come quickly. She did. We looked to see if we could see this character anywhere on the street but we didn't see hide nor hair of him.

MAZIE'S was open for three and one-half years. I finally had to close the shop when Mother became very ill. I just couldn't handle all the demands on me. I have never regretted having MAZIE'S. It was the first chance for me to have my own business and gave me a sense of security and independence. I think I developed a pretty good head for business. I learned the right questions to ask. I did my own books and learned about banking and about inventory control. I became an accomplished sole proprietor, a buyer, and a salesperson. I also learned how to work with and "handle the public."

I couldn't have asked for MAZIE'S to be any more than it was. It gave me a sense of direction after Daniel had "flown the nest." But, then again, I might have enjoyed the 'challenge' of becoming a chain store and making millions. Oh well, maybe one of these days!

Chapter 19

This chapter is about my mother, especially the last years of her life and my interaction with her. My mother died March 1997. She died from lung cancer that had spread to her brain. Prior to that, Mother had been diagnosed with emphysema and six month later she developed cancer. I believe that her many years of chain smoking contributed to both of these medical conditions.

Taking care of my mother was one of the events in my life that I did not question. It was an unconditional situation. I was only returning to her what she and Daddy had given to me. I cherish every day of those last two years when she moved to Sealy in 1994 to be near us. Thank goodness for my job working at "The Farm" with physically and mentally handicapped people. This job prepared me for the task ahead of me—taking care of Mother. This included my living with her at her apartment for nine months before she was moved to my home. Mother was no longer mentally or physically able to care for herself and the responsibility became mine.

Here it goes again-my support group. Jack, Steve, DeeDee, the doctors, Columbia Home Health, and a host of friends and relatives were there for me and for Mother. But, even with all this blessed support, in the end it was Mother and I who had to make it through, day-by-day, hour-by-hour. In the beginning of her illness I was going to her house three times a day. Mother had to use a breathing machine four times a day. She was weak and confused and even with the home health agency checking on here daily she wanted me. By July, she had been in and out of the hospital nine times.

The doctor verified emphysema. Her breathing became so difficult that I could see the look of fear in her eyes. It was time for me to drop everything and go to her. So, I did. This is when I moved in with her. It was very difficult for her to get from the bedroom to the bathroom, take her breathing treatment, or to eat. She had trouble remembering and was unsure about everything. But, you could see that small spark of determination in her. She was not ready to give in to this insidious disease.

She had turned over the banking and paying her bills to me. I tried to keep her informed about her business—her bills, banking, and buying. I wanted her to feel as though she was still participating in the daily act of living. She and I would laugh about the fact that her handwriting had become worse than mine. So at this juncture in my life my responsibilities included my business (Mazie's), my home, and my mother.

After Momma was diagnosed with lung cancer, I took her to a radiologist. He told us that she was not a good candidate for radiation. He did recommend an oncologist, Dr. Abramawitz. Our visit with him left us without too much hope. He told us that chemotherapy would not be a cure, but would give her more time. Mother and I had said for years that neither of us would ever take chemotherapy.

But, when it came right down to it, Mother decided to take the chemo because she was having such difficulty breathing. This was a decision I had to let her make on her own. We both knew what she would have to endure and I wanted her to be the one to make the final decision; I would support her no matter what her decision.

After her chemo, Mother still was not breathing any easier. They drained her lungs giving her more breathing capacity. The chemotherapy had left her so sick that I only left her bedside when another family member relieved me. I slept on a couch beside her bed. She always asked for a private room so someone could stay with her. This hospital stay was a little over one month.

One day I told her how long she had been in the hospital. A look of disbelief appeared on her face. I really don't think she had been aware of the length of time she had been this ill. I don't know if it was realizing the length of time or the cost of this length of time, but she began physical therapy immediately. We left the hospital within a week. Talk about one determined lady!

Ah the peace and quiet of home. The home health agency came in daily to bathe Momma and take vital signs. Numerous visitors and phone calls made life seem more normal. However, after five and one-half months of Momma and cancer, my energy level, along with my nerves, were on the low end of endurance.

With great sadness, I could see that Momma's life was nearing the end. I asked my husband, brother, and sister-in-law if we could move Momma to my house. I did not want to be alone when the end came.

The middle of February saw a very unusual sight in Sealy. It took seven of us to make the move, including our son, Daniel. He dearly loved his MeeMaw (that's what he called my momma) and wanted to participate in as much of her remaining life as he could. He came in from his home in Florida and was a great help with the move as well as a mental and emotional support for Momma and for me.

At my house, Jack cleaned out one bedroom, furniture and all. My brother, Steve, and his family (including his daughter's fiancée and his father) loaded all Momma's bedroom furniture including all the medical equipment she had accumulated. Then began a procession of cars and trucks from Momma's apartment to my house. Daniel and his MeeMaw followed.

After the move to my house, the doctor ordered Hospice. This service is called in when the doctor knows that the end is near. The social workers from Hospice are excellent in the care and information they provide. They also provide nurses and aides that saw to all of Momma's physical needs. Hospice also provides information on the stages of the dying process—a timetable of what to expect in the following weeks, days, and hours. This statement seems cold and harsh, but it was necessary for those of us who would be with Momma to the end. When you know what to expect, you can better handle, emotionally and physically, the situations that arise during the last days.

On the whole, Hospice was a blessing. However, at this point I must interject one unfortunate experience with one

141

member of Hospice. I do this, not to condemn Hospice as a whole, but to let readers know how one person affects another.

One morning, a hospice social worker was visiting with me. She asked if I would miss Mother since I needed Mother's support. I was taken aback and not real certain what she meant. I gasped and replied, "Yes! I will miss her terribly, as any daughter would." I further explained that I had been married for 28 years, raised a son, led a life with Jack, and had been independent of Momma for a long time. The woman must have seen my physical characteristics of CP and thought of me as being a weak person! Me! Mazie! Weak!

No matter how I tried to change the subject she would return to her questioning and try to elicit some self-pity. I refrained. She was so persistent with this topic that I almost asked her to leave. I kept my outward cool, but was seething on the inside.

Steve and his wife, DeeDee, were with us the first weekend in March. They left to go home, about a two-hour drive from Sealy. Jack and I were alone with Momma. Hospice had told us to keep talking to Momma. I spent the day sitting in her room talking to her, listening to hymns, and reading the paper.

I heard her breathing change. I called Jack. He explained that this is what occurs in the last phase. I continued to sit and watch.

A short while later, I heard her gasp. Again, I called in Jack. He leaned close to her, looked up with tears in his eyes and said, "Mazie, she is gone." Momma died March 2, 1997.

I was broken in a strange sort of way. I was sad, but there was a joy in my heart. As a Christian this is the way I believe it should be. I would miss Momma physically, but in my heart I knew she was with our Father. Momma's struggles were ended. Momma had told me she was ready. In fact, at one point she spoke to her own mother. She talked to family that had been dead for years. In a way, I was a little jealous. She was in a place for which I yearned…Heaven.

During Momma's illness I gained strength that I did not know I had. One never knows ones capacities until you are called on to pull from the bottom of your resources. I grew spiritually and learned what the family can and cannot do. Both Momma and I learned to live not one day at a time, but hour by hour. How precious is each hour. Sometimes these hours were filled with tears while others were filled with laughter—" the best of times and the worst of times."

I can't leave the story of Momma on a sad note. So, I have to tell an anecdote to illustrate the lighter side of Momma.

I needed to go to the store. I left Jack to tend to Momma. She needed to go into the bathroom, but did not let Jack know. She had a bell to ring, but I guess she didn't remember or didn't want to bother Jack. She made it to the bathroom and that is when Jack heard a thud. He hurried into the bathroom and there was Mother in the tub. She had become confused and instead of sitting on the toilet, she sat on the edge of the tub and fell in. Jack had to get into the tub and literally dance her out. I almost wish I had been there to see that!

As you might have noticed as you read this book I have been fortunate in my relationship with my parents. If it were possible, I would wish my parents on everyone. Unfortunately, I have lost both of them. They are no longer in this physical world but I have them next to me and in my heart always.

Chapter 20

"Lord you have given me a mountain ... I cannot climb"

In 1993 my life changed one more time. I have forever lost the feeling of being secure and wrapped in the arms of financial security. After 13 years with Conoco, Jack was laid off. Our financial security dissolved. For the first time in my life I questioned God and asked, "Why Me?"

Why me? Hadn't I always accepted what He had given me? Hadn't I taken those valleys along with all the mountains placed in front of me? I had never questioned Him before. He gave me what I know saw as an insurmountable obstacle. I could not soar like an eagle with this blow.

I was mad at Conoco, at God, and at the world. Jack had made cutbacks for a number of years so we thought we were safe. Wrong! I had faith that God would protect US from this devastation that seemed to be crossing the United States. Jack was 47 years old and making a high salary. He was a prime candidate for a lay off.

We found ourselves in a financial bind. Daniel was attending Texas Tech in Lubbock, Texas. We had his college education in savings, thanks to his grandparents. Otherwise, we would not have had the money for him to continue his education. However, as all parents, we could not say no to our son or our community. Therefore our credit card debt was stretched to the limit.

This was a very lonely time in our life. I found myself asking, "Where are my friends?" Most of our friends knew of our loss of job and our son being away from home. At first we received invitation to go out, but this took money. We had to decline because we had bills to pay. After about six months we were unable to do anything with our friends. A number of them quit asking us; some saw our hurt and asked us over for dinner and cards. We could do that. Guilt would then set in because I could not afford to reciprocate. The band and speech boosters went their way. I took comfort in saying that these friends went on to doing other activities. Out of sight, out of mind—surely they cared what was happening to us, but—!

Jack worked hard at trying to land a job. He went to the job help office Conoco had for the many people they let go. This was about the only good Conoco did for all the devastation to human lives they caused. Jack made a 40-hour a week job out of looking for a job—with little success. He did this for 18 months. This was very had to watch—interview after interview. He had too much experience for the salary being offered, not in his field computer-wise (in other words no experience in the type of software they used) these were the answers Jack would get when he interviewed. One week he had three to five possibilities. We became excited trying to determine which would be better for him. Then he would get a call saying, "I'm sorry.. . ." –you can fill in the rest. This went on for months—mountains of high hopes, valleys of rejection and despair. It was a living hell for me. Jack was able to cope better than I because he was around others who were in the same situation. I was by myself. We were an isolated family unable to meet our financial needs and responsibilities. Our marriage was rocky; our faith was rocky. It was a good thing we started this plunge with a solid marriage and solid faith or otherwise this story would have a different ending.

Jack found only contract work in computer drafting for oil companies. We have had no benefits—no 401K, no insurance. We had to carry our own private policy along with life insurance. It wasn't until 1999 that we were relieved of this burden when I was promoted at my job at Willow River Farm. Even now when I am no longer working for Willow River Farm paying privately covers us.

In 1995 Jack quit working as a drafter and bought a screen printing business. He was already producing shirts for our son's band and shirts for plays, program covers and tickets. We had never owned our own business and had no doubt that this would be the way to ease our financial situation. Little did we know how much it would take out of us. Jack worked long hours. Even with the help of one employee, there were not enough hours in the day for the two of them to accomplish all that had to be done. They had to take orders, design the artwork, do color separations (usually at home, at night, after an exhausting day at work) chasing after the supplies, and manually silk-screening. It was just too much.

Another defeat. The business was not paying our living expenses. In March 1996 Jack was forced to close the business. It was a stressful time in our lives and in our marriage. The lack of money and the pure physical toll was almost too much. I had always looked at our marriage as being a strong marriage. But, we had never had these overwhelming obstacles and defeats. It took all we had to hold our marriage together.

My life had never been tried in so many ways before so stretched beyond my control. I was in my mid-forties. I had cerebral palsy. My only son had left home and I had an empty nest. My husband, also in his 40's, was without work and mentally and physically worn out. I was running my shop, Mazie's, almost single-handed. My mother had moved to Sealy and was in deteriorating health. And to top it all off – Daniel decided to place his college on hold and go to work in Florida for the Disney Company. My colitis returned with a vengeance!

The death of my momma seemed to be the straw that would break the camel's back. I could not handle all of the overwhelming misery that I felt. Why did I feel so lonely and empty when for so long I had depended upon my support group. Where had it gone? It seemed to become weaker and weaker as more and more everyday life became overwhelming to me.

By Christmas of 1997 I became so ill I was hospitalized. I thought I was dying. I was on Prozac, for depression. The doctor sent me for a gynecologist for hormone therapy and to a gastroenterologist for my colon problems. I was hospitalized three times. I did not do well being alone. I convinced myself that I was dying. I was having some of the same symptoms and same procedures that Momma had. I felt that the outcome would be the same—death. I had so many memories of the past years and I was totally unhappy.

I relied on talking to Daniel for some relief of my misery. One of the times I was in the hospital I called his pager number. It was a voice pager and I left the message, "I am in the hospital. I need to hear your voice." In whatever manner this was conveyed to Daniel, whether electronically or by a person, it went through three times. My desperation must have been apparent.

Just when I thought I had nothing to live for, my support group kicked in again. My husband, son, brother, sister-in-law, father-in-law, mother-in-law, and many friends held me close. Sometimes it was physically close sometimes it was emotionally close. This is what I needed to heal me in both my body and mind. God works in mysterious ways—of this I am certain. He brought me back into my belief through my family. I still had the lingering feeling that my final destination is near.

So I began writing this book. Maybe Carman is trying to extend what I thought would be my 'swan song,' because I was ready to finish this book in six months and now it has been three years.

I must have put on a pretty good "outside" appearance. Jerome, a dear friend, confirmed this when he wrote, "I feel that Mazie has had an unusual life with difficult times. But what makes Mazie unusual is the way she handles life. She makes it look easier than I know it really is."

Maybe this was why not all of my friends knew the agony and misery I felt. I received a letter from one friend, Tim Ward, who said, "I felt so sorry for you because of the tremendous responsibility you were laboring under.... It must have been a devastating time in your life and you handled it with such aplomb and cheerfulness."

Since the end of 1996 Jack has been working contract jobs. The jobs have been with various companies. For the last 18 months he has been at the same company. Still, we have no benefits. Please understand I'm not complaining because I thank God we are financially better off now. Jack has developed a greater sense of his abilities, but he and I would still like to have job security. This day and age, however, there is a different attitude and climate in the working world.

My faith, my self, my soul, my marriage, my life has improved. Not that I don't still have down times, but I know "this too will pass."

Chapter 21

I appreciate all Jack does for me. I also appreciate how much he cares—even concerning the writing of *Mazie's Mountain*. After thirty-three years of marriage I was greatly surprised at how much he remembers about our dating years. It brought tears to my eyes. As to how and what he wrote—here it is for you to enjoy.

Jack's Version of My Life

I guess I can blame the life I now lead on Alexander Graham Bell because I first met Mazie over the phone. The first time I heard Mazie talk I thought I had a drunk on the phone. I had called my current girlfriend and she had to leave the phone for a few minutes. Oh what those few minutes did to my life. As Mazie has said earlier in this tome, I asked my girlfriend who the drunk was and she reamed me out, but good. She let me know that her friend has CP and I should not be so inconsiderate. My girlfriend and I reached a truce when I told her that I was expressing that I thought she sounded like she was drunk, not that she was a drunk.

I finally met Mazie when we had a "dual" birthday party. Since my birthday is the day after Mazie's a few of our friends decided to celebrate our birthdays together. During the evening, all the guys danced with the birthday girl and of course I fulfilled my obligation. I must add that I made sure we danced to something slow since that was all I could handle. During the dance I sensed that she seemed nervous. When I asked if she were nervous, she said that she wasn't nervous, but shakes involuntarily. Gee, she could have made my night and said something about being so affected by being in my arms that she was "all shook-up". But, something interesting did happen. Mazie was wearing a shaggy sweater and it became caught on my tie tack. Yes, way back then we wore shirts and ties on dates! Anyway, to make a long story short, hoots and comments accompanied the "untangling" of our clothes. "Oh what a tangled web we weave" when we dance close!

The next time I had close contact with Mazie was when the Newman Club planned a joint swimming party and picnic with the Club from Stephen F. Austin College in Nacogdoches, Texas. This was our only contact for quite some time. I quit attending the Newman Club and went about my way. Later, I ran in to Mazie and when she asked what I'd been up to (as anyone might ask someone they hadn't seen in some time) I became very defensive and said I'd been busy. The defensive attitude had nothing to do with her. I was having some Catholic guilt about not attending Mass or going to the Newman Club. I really felt lousy about this and later called her to apologize. For some reason, that phone call lasted much longer than I had originally intended – as well as the results of that call.

We dated for a couple of years. I wish I could say that it was heaven. Actually it was more like sailing. We definitely had our ups and downs. We had a lot of differences to overcome. I was the typical, broke, unkempt art major and she was the neatnic Home Economics major. Also, both of us had some growing up to do, I probably had more to do than she did. At one point, I thought our relationship was finished. We were upset with each other and Mazie wanted out, although I didn't. We met at the Lowman Student Center on campus to try and resolve many issues. I'll never forget—Mazie dressed appropriately in black. Both of us were crying. Suddenly, over the sound system came the song "I've Grown Accustomed to Her Face" and both of us melted. We decided that what we had was worth giving it another shot.

Later that year, after one of our coke dates (and I mean Coca Cola), it struck me that I was really serious about Mazie. I decided I'd better do something before I lost her. As soon as I got home after dropping her at her dorm, I called her up and asked her to meet me in a few minutes. I'm sure she thought I was nuts because we'd just spent the evening together. She was full of questions but I wouldn't tell her anything other than that I needed to talk to her. It took only a few minutes to get back to the dorm. There we were, sitting in the car, with me becoming more and more nervous. I guess this was my time to be the one shaking, not Mazie. I told her, "I love you. Will you marry me?" To this day I assume she said yes. I honestly don't remember. However, she did accept the engagement ring that I gave her later that summer. Things really moved fast after that commitment. As far as I was concerned, our senior year flew by. We were planning a wedding for August 3, her dad's birthday.

Mazie's family was and continues to be great. I have never felt as comfortable with anyone as I did with Mazie and her family. Her mother, Louise, was a scream. She was an eternal chatterbox and chain smoker. I guess she and her husband, Neal, were well suited since he was the quiet type and could probably have never gotten a word in edgewise anyway. However, when he did say something, you would make a point to listen.

As any married man will tell you, I guess the wedding went off without a hitch. However, I can't say the same for the honeymoon. Now I know that with Mazie having cerebral palsy and the shakes people have an interest as to whether or not we can have a "normal" physical life. Well, let me tell you this. I won't go into the really "good" stuff, but Mazie doesn't shake when she is relaxed. Of course I have no other woman with whom to compare physical activity, but as far as I am concerned, Mazie is as normal physically as any other woman. Notice, I did put the adjective "physically" in there. Anyway, back to the honeymoon. As I said, her mother was a real card. Louise and her neighbor had sewn up Mazie's nightgown across the bottom with a chain stitch and filled it, and her other clothes, with rice. Well, there we were at the motel and Mazie had gone into the bathroom to change. Within minutes, she was having a fit and laughing very hard. That was real good for my ego. Was she laughing at me? At what was coming? What???? Mazie couldn't get into her nightgown and rice was everywhere. Of course, as things turned out, she didn't need the gown anyway. Whew! I wonder how we would have explained that one if she hadn't even tried to get it on? The next morning, we called her parents. Mazie tried to read the riot act to her mother, but before the conversation had gotten very far, we were all laughing so hard we had tears in our eyes.

This was the year that the Viet Nam War was going full bore. Within two months of graduation I received my draft notice. I had had a student deferment but that was over. I received my summons from the Selective Service and went for the battery of tests. They told me that I had high blood pressure and was overweight (240 lbs.). I would receive a temporary deferment, but would be recalled the following year for another physical. True to their word, a year later I had to undergo another physical. However, by this time I had lost 75 pounds. Mazie's mom had gone on Weight Watcher's and asked me if I wanted to join her in going to the meetings. I agreed and lost the weight. This became a mixed blessing when I went in for my second physical. Now my weight was under control and I figured this would also take care of the high blood pressure. However, it didn't. I still had extremely high blood pressure and was reclassified as 4F. After this, I went to a doctor for the blood pressure. I guess I had never taken high blood pressure as a serious problem, but I did now. With medication I was able to bring it under control. Don't misunderstand me. Even though I detested the war and knew I didn't want to waste my life on it, I also knew if called, I would serve. My Dad was a career Air Force pilot on active duty, at the time, and I understood duty.

157

Mazie and I took the advice of friends and decided that we needed to take at least a year to get to know each other better before having children and the responsibilities and distractions of parenthood. However, years passed by with no luck once we did make the decision to conceive. We finally went to see Mazie's gynecologist. He ran tests on both of us. Mazie had a tubal problem and I had a slight prostrate infection causing a low sperm count. My infection was easily and quickly corrected. But, Mazie's was not that easy to correct. In reality, it meant that she could only get pregnant every other month.

Mazie's doctor was an interesting character with a sly sense of humor and genuinely cared about his patients. After all the testing and discussions, he said he loved working with couples that had fertility problems. He said he would do everything in his power to get us "on the road to procreation." "What is procreation?" Mazie leaned over and asked me as we left his office. I nearly fell over I laughed so hard. I asked if she was serious. She answered, a little on the testy side, "Of course I am. I've never heard that word procreation before." She was a little embarrassed after I told her that it was a fancy way of saying having children. We giggled about it all the way home. Still, it took more than a year for "us" to get pregnant. During that time,

Mazie had to try to forget about having children and concentrate on other things. She became involved in the community. Then a miracle took place. IT happened. After years of feeling sorry for herself, crying, and both of us trying too hard, she had gotten wrapped up in others' problems and forgot about her own. I've heard of this happening to other couples too. Who knows if that is the real reason, but it is as good of explanation as any.

There are several moments in a couple's life together that they remember more than any other. The sheer joy and excitement of learning you are expecting your first child, the trip to the hospital when labor starts, and the day that child comes into your life as a living, breathing, helpless bundle. The next most memorable moment comes when you gather up all of your belongings at the hospital, take your new son in your arms and head for home for the first time. You walk in the door and realize that, from now on you both are responsible for a new life and you don't know diddley squat how to go about doing it. Abject fear sets in. How do you do this? How do you do that? Are we feeding him too much? Are we feeding him the right formula? Is it the right temperature? Are we changing him often enough? Is he warm enough? Is he sleeping in the right position? What was that noise?

I need to backtrack a bit, to when Mazie went into labor. A few weeks before, I had a weird dream that we were going to the hospital and her water broke in the car. What a mess! When I got the call to come home to take Mazie to the hospital, I remembered the dream and grabbed a garbage bag and put it over the seat before she got in the car. Talk about getting some grief. I just figured once warned, twice shy. Enough about my odd mind and me. At the hospital, things went fine. We got there about 3:30 pm and Daniel was born about 7:30 pm. Mazie's parents came by about two hours after we got there. As usual, Louise was a chatterbox, Neal, however, was fun to watch, if you knew what to watch for. On the outside, Neal was as calm and cool as ever. On the inside, he was a bundle of nerves. He constantly paced the whole floor. He also had a pocket full of change that he rattled continually. Kind of reminded me of Humphrey Bogart as Capt. Queeg rolling his ball bearings, in "The Caine Mutiny." He didn't stop moving until the nurses announced that Mazie had given birth.

After they brought out Daniel and we got to see him for the first time, we went in to see Mazie for a minute before they took her to her room. Dr. Freundlich came in and told us everything went fine. He then wheeled Mazie out to her room on the gurney while whistling "Onward Christian Soldiers." Funny thing to whistle. Even funnier since he is Jewish.

Life went on from that point. Raising Daniel, buying a new house, meeting new neighbors, getting involved in the community and church—all the things that every normal family goes through. Mazie never stumbled. Her condition never got in the way, or, at least, she never let on that it did. Sure, I had to button the occasional button or put on the odd earring back for her. But, I'm talking about whatever life brought her. Getting around, working with people, and just trying to keep body and soul together. Her CP was only a problem for other people. When Mazie joined the local garden club, she experienced quite a bit of standoffishness from some of the other women in the club. They were put-off by this strange, to them, woman who shook and had an odd speaking voice. Within a few months, they could have cared less that Mazie had any unusual physical condition. All it took was for them to be around her, see how hard she worked, her organizing abilities and how creative she was, to realize that they were the ones with the problem and not Mazie. A year later Mazie was elected President of the garden club.

This is the effect Mazie has. People are uncomfortable at first contact. It puts them with their own fears. "What's wrong with her? Can't she talk right? Why does she walk that way? Is what she has, catching? Should I protect my children? She has a son? What kind of a man would touch her? Watch out, her son might be just like her. Watch for the signs." That is what goes through people's minds—especially people who are insecure and ignorant. People who have been raised to think that different is bad, that strange is to be avoided at all costs. It's like the poor fools who think they have to shout in order for a blind person to hear them.

The cure? Knowledge! Contact! As often as possible. I guess you could say I've been blessed, up to a point. Her condition never even fazed me. Perhaps it was because she was a friend of a friend. Perhaps it was because I met her in college and not on the street. Perhaps it had to do with my own upbringing. Whatever the answer is, I can tell you one thing: It doesn't matter a hill of beans and neither did her physical situation. From time to time, for more than thirty years, Mazie asks me if I love her. My answer is always the same. Yes! Which always brings up next question. "How do you know?" My answer is, again, always the same. "Because I just do." I can't enumerate reasons. I can't tick off characteristics like a shopping list. It stems from a decision I made a long time ago and I am happy to live with it and her.

Mazie, I love you!

Chapter 22

Daniel, our bundle of joy, also wrote. It was once again a total surprise when I read what he wrote. He is now in his mid-twenties and living on his own. As I said before, our children are a true gift from God. Hold them close because we only have them a short while.

I believe the two lasting gifts we can give our children are one's roots and the other is wings. Daniel, I hope your daddy and I have given you these two gifts.

Enjoy reading Daniel's writing about his life with me.

I never really realized that all mothers weren't like mine until I was in the fourth or fifth grade. That's when my classmates began asking me things like: "Is she okay?" or "Why is she so upset all the time?" Then, I had to take a long, hard look at her to see what they were talking about. I'm sure there were some people who avoided being around Momma because of her physical attributes. However, sitting here today, I can't think of a single person who made that known to me—or their opinions were so insignificant that I didn't pay them any attention.

Actually, I recall people saying things like, "You can never forget Mazie." or, "She makes a strong impression." Most of my friends said the same thing: "I love your mom."

I think she draws this response because of her wonderful personality. Initially, new acquaintances must adjust to her physical traits. They quickly find that they are won over by her friendly, southern personality. I think that aspects of Momma's personality helped to teach me how to avoid having problems with my peers. She showed me through her actions that the more outgoing and comfortable you are around new people—whether or not they are comfortable around you—the more apt they are to at least understand that your intentions are good. Her direct and somewhat "in-your-face" demeanor can force people to communicate with her, talk to her and not at her, and confront the stigma of dealing with someone who is different. By being (or playing) the eternal extrovert, others are not given a chance to become afraid or shy away from her. Her questions and animated conversations tend to put a swift end to any attempts to avoid her. I do not think any of these characteristics are a part of someone having cerebral palsy. But, I do believe that they arose from it. It is her way of adapting to her surroundings. I have watched people from 3-year-olds to 80-year-olds begin by being

165

startled by her movements and quickly transition into a warm conversation with her. That's why so many people feel comfortable talking to Momma.

Despite what others may have perceived, her shaking never embarrassed me. It is difficult to explain, but I very rarely notice the shaking. I have always been aware of her reaction to people and situations, though. If the situation is difficult, confusing or causes her stress, she will outwardly display her stress by shaking. The defensive only child in me wants to calm her down or remove the source of the stress—but that says more about my personality than hers.

Even though I can almost certainly say that her shaking didn't embarrass me as a child, her boisterous communication style is another matter. Her outgoing and sometimes loud personality gave me much frustration as a teenager (much the way that the woman in the Phillip's Milk of Magnesia commercial begins talking about her embarrassed husband's constipation to a fellow customer in the drug store). I think all of us know someone who can talk to anyone they meet. Well, you can count on my mother to talk to the person in line at the grocery store, the person sitting in the theatre next to you and just about anyone else she can hold still. So many times my mother has told some complete stranger intimate details of my life as I scuffed my feet and hid around the corner. You aren't loosing your mind. Just a minute ago, I did say that her outgoing personality is her strongest trait. Just like all strengths, being too outgoing can also be a weakness—especially for a 13-year-old who becomes the captive topic of conversation with a complete stranger!

It is often difficult for me to watch Momma's frustration when she is unable to perform a task. Sometimes the task is as simple as opening a bottle of soda. Her emotions flow right into her physical movements. Any control over her body that she possesses is lost when she becomes stressed, confused or self-conscious. But again, this bothers me; it doesn't embarrass me. It was frustrating at times to be forced to stand by as the grocery clerk repeatedly offered to help my mother with writing her check or as a department store clerk looked on as my mother signed the charge card receipt. It was difficult to sit by as my mother strained to speak clearly enough at the drive-through window or try to communicate to someone that was upsetting her. I'm sure I could be found looking away or avoiding eye contact with those around me.

Sometimes while I was growing up she would scold me for

doing something or saying something she didn't like—as with any child. Just as any son or daughter, I would react by mocking her I'm sure. To the outsider it would seem that I was mocking her shakes or frustrated speech to be cruel—to get at her. As I'm sure it angered other adults around her, the reactions I had to her were the same, as those any child would have to being scolded or chided for misbehavior. To me, mocking my mother's physical characteristics was the same as my friends repeating their mother's objections in a mocking voice. That's the way kids are.

Granted my relationship with my parents was strained during my teen-age years—whose isn't. I probably wasn't the ideal son that everyone would have liked me to be. I know that I was more frank with my parents than many of my friends were with theirs. I can only attribute this to my lack of siblings. My parents always treated me as an equal part of the family. I watched so many of my multiple-sibling friends lack the input or influence that I was given in my family. My mother and I developed a stronger relationship because of this. She didn't demand more of me than to be her friend. So many of my friends' parents seemed to demand a rigid distance of respect and discipline that I was never subject to (incidentally, almost all of my friends had brothers and sisters). My mother was my friend as a child and even as a teenager. As long as I wasn't too out of line, she would tolerate more from me in terms of disciplinary problems than the average parent would. I started noticing this as I entered high school. Since I wasn't a wild child, I think I passed through most of my high school years without incident. I had more problems with my dad during this period (actually during most of my childhood) than I did with my mother—I'm not sure why.

The most embarrassing thing that I've had to deal with regarding my mother rarely takes place when she is present. Her handwriting has always been a challenge to read. I've been unable to read notes she wrote me all my life. Teachers would often ask about her writing in front of other students. One such situation took place when I was in high school. I think I was a sophomore at the time. The schools in Sealy were so behind the times that they still had individual grade cards (hand-written no less) for each class. We would return them to each teacher after our parents had signed them. My Spanish teacher was particularly thoughtless and lacking tact in the way she spoke to students. She evoked what I think is the strongest response that I have ever given regarding my mother's condition. This teacher liked to call you up one at a time to turn in your report card. She would check it off in her grade book after reviewing it. You would then be sent back to your seat. My name was called and I took my card to her and waited as all the other students did. She then looked at the card and hesitated. She looked at me and said, in a nasal and very loud tone, "Senor, Daniel do you consider this a joke?" To which I responded, "What?" Truly clueless to what she was talking about, after all—the grade was an 'A.' "Do you expect me to believe that this was signed by your parent? Whose signature is this suppose to be?" Remember, this entire conversation is taking place at normal speaking volume and in front of the entire class of 25 of my peers—many of whom knew my mother well. I was so stunned by her flagrant disregard to my privacy and my mother that I responded in an angry voice, "That is my mother's signature." She looked at me and chuckled, "Well, if my mother had handwriting like this, I would bring her to school to learn how to write more legibly." The class then began to murmur and whisper, as they all knew my mother's condition. I felt myself becoming red in the face and shaking with anger. I breathed deeply and said in a quiet voice, fighting off my anger, "My mother has cerebral palsy." She didn't look up from her podium or even hint at an apology. Given that she had just insulted me to the core, I stormed out of the classroom and walked down to the administration office. I spoke with one of the school administrators about what had just happened. This person knew my mother and was equally outraged. We walked back down to the classroom and the administrator called out the teacher to explain the situation. We demanded that she apologize to me and to the class for her insensitivity. The teacher, however, denied having taken more than a passing glance at the signature even though 25 of my classmates had been witness to her uncouth comments. I told my parents about what had happened when I got home from school. My mother, taking a humorous account of the situation said she would consider sending her a note in her handwriting just to see if she could decipher it. To this day, I think my mother was reacting with humor as a defense to the real pain that it must have caused her. I doubt that this teacher even remembers the situation. I, on the other hand, have her insensitive words burned into my mind.

Another situation surrounding Momma's handwriting took place when I was much younger. I don't recall the precise year or my age, but I know that I was in elementary school. We had gone shopping for groceries at a Kroger in Houston. We spent about an hour picking out our purchases. My mother walked up to the checkout and began filling out her check as the clerk finished ringing her items into the register. I noticed the clerk's glances at my mother's gyrations as she wrote out her check. The clerk then read the total aloud and waited wincing as my mother filled out the dollar amount. My mother then carefully tore the check out of her checkbook and handed it to the clerk whom I remember as a young woman. The woman then looked at my mother's driver's license and said, "Ma'am, we can't take this. Do you have another method of payment?" My mother said in a stressed voice, "What's wrong with my check? You took it last time." The clerk responded, "I can't read this. How do you expect us to cash it?" My mother then sharply asked for her manager. Rolling her eyes, the clerk called her manager. The manager came over and told her the same thing. My mother said, "I have CP. Do you know what that is?" The manager said, "No, ma'am, I don't." My mother responded loudly, "Well, until you figure it out, I'll take my business elsewhere!" She took my hand and stormed out the door. I remember wondering who would put away all of the eight or nine bags of groceries we had spent an hour selecting. My mother was very shaken and very upset by this entire episode. To this day, I don't think that my mother or my family will shop in that chain—or at least at that store

Her unique combination of facing life with humor and her determined attitude has made my mother an inspiration to me. She gave me her outgoing personality and a love of conversation. She has given everyone that she touches something. Sometimes she gives a good laugh and sometimes she gives the comfort of a shoulder to cry on. So many people have commented, "I love your mother." It makes me realize that I don't tell her enough how much she means to me. She may stress me out—what mother doesn't do that every now and then—but she is still the best mother that I could have.

Chapter 23

"True friends give you their opinions, false ones give you yours."

Richard C. Miller

Carman told me that she did not remember her childhood. Wrong...note the length of this chapter. As I stated in the acknowledgments, I have a dear and close friend, I still cherish after all these years. Thank you for writing this book with me. Now we can claim to be playmates, sole mates, and co-authors. Carman and Mazie, what a special relationship—one that can be picked up where it left off. I say this because we had gone twelve or so years out of touch, then after we 'reconnected' we would go months at a time without connecting. Now, in writing Mazie's Mountain, it has been quite frequent, weeks and now days.

Today, it is as if we are playmates again because we are involved in writing and making decisions. Carman's mother and husband have had to listen while we discussed, cussed, and giggled—as we did when we were young girls.

I appreciate their patience and support. Now, here is Carman's long chapter.

The following is Carman's contribution to this book concerning her remembrance of our childhood together as well as comments about "life after Eagle Lake."

I think that we have been friends through thick and thin. Unfortunately, I have more thick than thin. Maybe that is what makes a friendship endure as long as ours. Even though I am older, it doesn't necessarily mean I am wiser or more diplomatic, but here goes. Well, Mazie, I'm not too sure you want to hear everything I have to say. You know better than to ask my opinion, since you did asked, here goes.

I really don't remember much about our Eagle Lake years. I guess that was so long ago. I don't remember your "handicap" ever affecting our play but it sure did affect my feelings about you periodically. For example, remember the day we moved from the old school to the brand new elementary school? We had to walk and carry all of our supplies from our desks. I was walking with you, of course. BUT---about a block from the school, you were given a ride and I had to continue to walk in the heat and humidity and carry OUR supplies. Talk about "pushing the limits of friendship!"

Also, remember that dance recital where I was to be the "STAR?" or that was my perception, and I became very ill. Of course, you took my place! I know it wasn't your fault, but that didn't compute, as they say, at the time. I wanted to be the elephant trainer and lead the parade. I really wanted to crack that whip over the elephant, my brother. (*Here, again, is another story about your parents doing what was right—enrolling you in dance—which is the type of motor skill development needed by everyone who has cerebral palsy.*)

We have talked about your family and your relationship with them. I remember your mother teaching the Brownies to miter the corners of the sheet when we made it up, which was long before contoured sheets. And, I remember the cook-out in the pasture behind your house. I still think that was one of the best meals I've ever eaten. However, in reality, it was probably really, really, bad. I mean after all, how good could a meal be when it was cooked in a one-pound coffee can and buried in the coals. I also remember the time you spent the night with me, and I ended up with my hand in "urp" and dill pickle.

I also have a different memory of your brother Steve. When you talk about him now, as you remember him, you always speak of him in glowing and loving terms. What I remember about him is that he was seldom around when I was around you. And, when we were around him, he threatened us with our lives to not go into his room. He never treated you any differently than my older sister treated me. I never remember your being given special treatment because of your cerebral palsy (which we didn't know you had).

That does jog my memory on one other subject. I remember your going to Houston and having to come home and make a scrapbook. I was so hurt because I couldn't help you with it. The nerve!!! Of course back then I didn't understand why. I just knew that we always did everything together and here was something so special and I could not participate.

I remember your living in Westbury; however, I don't remember the move or how it affected me although I'm certain it must have. I know that a separation of interests began after the split in our lives and so it continued for these many years.

I remember our "hooking up" again when my husband, my two children and I moved back to Eagle Lake. You, Jack, and Daniel were living in Houston at the time. It was a hit and miss relationship because both of us were so busy with our families. I do remember talking to my children before they met you. I wanted them to understand about your "handicap" because I did not want to embarrass you by their asking rude questions when they met you. I thought I had made them understand about cerebral palsy, but I guess I didn't do such a good job of explaining.

When I asked my daughter about meeting you, the only thing she remembers is that she really, really hated your dogs—sorry about that! My son, on the other hand, had a very definite impression of your having "SOMETHING." He was very apologetic when he e-mailed me the information. He said to make certain that you understood that he was young and probably should have asked more questions. But, of course he didn't. He said he remembers being afraid to eat anything at your house or to use your utensils, or the bathroom, etc. because he was afraid he would "catch it."

Here is his e-mail:

> I have been asked to write down my recollection of my mother's friend Mazie. I am not entirely happy about doing this. The reason being that when I dredged up the memories I realized that at a young age, not even knowing what the word meant, I held a prejudice. I question it only for the fact that I'm unsure of the word to properly describe my feelings. My first memories of her were of only wanting to keep my distance from her, and to this day I can't put my finger on exactly why, only that I was uncomfortable around her. My memory has been faulty in the past and this may be

another case, but I don't recall my parents explaining what was different about her until much later (a few years), or maybe they did and I didn't understand until later.

Now trying to explain, (and now that I'm writing this, trying to understand), feelings that I had over 20 years ago, that even then I couldn't have explained. As I write this I realize that my parents must have tried an explanation or two or three since I now remember not wanting to eat from their utensils or flatware for fear of ending up like her. There I said it all. I can only hope that she [Mazie] can forgive a young, and I will say ignorant human for any pain that I caused in the past and any that I may cause by my writings. She is one of the sweetest most patient people that I know. Now that I'm older and a little wiser, I can truthfully say, one of the strongest. If I ever suffer what she has suffered and can maintain even a portion of her cheerfulness and a smidgen of her strength, I will consider myself fortunate.

Kenneth E. Wiese
Staff Sergeant United States Army

Lord, Mazie, I wish I had known that. I would have certainly explained a little better. Do you have many experiences with children having that perception?

Kenneth wants me to reassure you, if you need to be reassured, that his admiration for you and what you have accomplished knows no bounds. He says this from an adult perspective and from one who has to get the best from the soldiers under his command. So, he knows what limitations or perceived limitations can do to a person. He said that evidently you do not perceive yourself to have limitations.

Of course, this brings me to another point. This may ruin our friendship. I certainly hope not. But, you've been saying that everyone has such glowing things to say about you and that you want to know the truth. Well, here goes. I do admire you greatly and you have been an inspiration to me. Anytime I think I can't do something, because of any limitation I perceive I have, I think about the time in the ceramic shop. Do you remember? I was concerned about your being around so many breakable objects and doing such intricate work on them. You just smiled and said, "Well, if I break one, I just start over." Damn! I could have done without that!!! You could have given me some great philosophical explanation. But, no, you just said, "I just start over." However, although this admiration for you has not diminished, you are still a pain in the butte sometimes and you hurt my feelings by your comments.

I know that you and Jack have more "artistic" creativity than I, but our tastes in home decorations will never meet. I really like my old (even though it may not officially be classified as antique) furniture. You and Jack are good matches and you have to remember that my relationship with my husband works for us, just as yours with Jack works for you. I know that what you see in our marriage is only the "moment in time" that you are there. You react to my action or words toward my husband without knowing the cause for them. When negative comments are made about this relationship, it puts a barrier between you and me. Remember, that old Indian saying about don't make judgments until you walk in someone else's shoes? I say this because I do not want the people who read your book to gag on the "goodness and admiration" you invoke. To me you are more like a sister. I love you for what you are, but darn, you can be stubborn, hard headed, focused only on your wants and needs (as anybody can be and is at times, even me) or, as Daniel said, you get an idea or plan and you just railroad people into doing it your way. Are you able to accomplish so much because people feel sorry for you and do not want to inhibit anything you try because it would not be politically correct? Or is it because of the railroading business? Personally, I think it is the railroading personality and you would accomplish whatever you want, no matter what! I will have to have you take the Myers/Briggs Test!!!

(I looked up railroading and what it really means is you push through, rush, expedite, speed up, quicken, accelerate, hurry or

hasten events. But, of course, how else do you get people "up and
at 'em"?)

OK, of course I have to add all the wonderful, thoughtful, considerate (is that syrupy enough?) things you have done for me. When I had surgery and was in the hospital in Houston, you came and sat in my room. My family was "too busy" to come, but not you. In fact, I remember your being the one to make the nurse remove the trachea tube because I kept gagging. "Get in here and remove this tube. She keeps gagging." I think you intimidated all of the staff. You also told the nurses, "Take better care of my friend."

When Judy, my sister, died, you offered me the sanctuary of your home. You waited for me to arrive, offered your hospitality, sociable but didn't asked questions, or expect me to be—no questions, just "we're here when you need us."

I used to become very angry with Daniel when he would roll his eyes while you were speaking or when he thought you were taking too long to complete a task or he would mock your movements. I now know that it was because he was a teenager and this was his way of coping. But, sometimes, I just wanted to shake him and yell at him, "You think you could do this?" but because of my respect for you and Jack I never did. I usually just went home very angry.

I am still angry that the doctors didn't diagnose cerebral palsy when you were younger. The years you lived with "all you have to do is try harder" was a crock. I'm glad you knew you were doing your best.

I've been thinking about the story you told about the college psychology professor who advised you about your future career; he must have been an academician, not an educator. The very nerve!!!!!!!

PHEW! That was more than I was expecting. I wonder what she meant by my hurting her feelings. You know; she's not Miss Goody-Two-Shoes herself. I guess we're going to have to have a long conversation about this.

Chapter 24

JOHN and his mom, Mary

Ahhh, what can I say about John. He was like a brother to me. When I contacted him about writing this book he was as supportive as ever. I told him that I wanted the truth, no holds barred. Carman contacted him and told him the same thing.

Because our paths never crossed at a time convenient for both of us, I never had the opportunity to personally visit with him. But, he was able to return Carman's phone call and discuss our relationship.

When John was asked what terms he would use to describe Mazie when they were growing up together Carman got a good laugh when he used the terms "hard-headed and bossy." She told him that is what she had said about me also. He said that he hated to disappoint Mazie if she were expecting him to feel that he had overcome any qualms about having her as a friend or if he should have felt that he needed to defend or explain her "condition" in any way. "I never felt sorry for Mazie. Mazie is just Mazie." That was one phrase he used over and over, "Mazie is just Mazie."

The name Mazie was given to me by John. As you have read my story you have seen how important that name has been to me and to my self esteem. John gave me more than just friendship. Enjoy reading his comments.

Mazie never used her "problem" as an excuse, the way that many people seem to want to do today. I never looked at her as feeling sorry for her and I sure didn't cater to her. I probably received more from our relationship than she did because she taught me jacks, hopscotch and other games and, I might add, she was pretty darn good at them too. Also, Mazie had and still has a good sense of humor. But, she was like all of us, if she didn't get her way, she would scream and holler.

I believe one of the main reasons that I never thought of Mazie as "being different" is because my parents never made a big deal out of it. If they ever had comments to make about her "condition" it was never, ever said in my presence. But, I really doubt if they thought much about the difference. When you grow up with someone, you accept or reject them for what they are and what they do. I, of course, accepted Mazie. I never remember anyone labeling Mazie as anything other than "a friend", no adjectives or explanations needed or used.

Well, that does sound just like John!

MARY HIGHT

(John's mother and my long time friend)

I first knew Mazie when she was four, maybe five, years old. This was at the Shaver home in Eagle Lake where I was studying pottery, a course taught by Mazie's mother, Louise. Mazie was a frail looking child, with the dearest smile one can imagine. She did not run as fast or yell as much as other kids, but I soon learned she was anything but 'frail.' Even though her voice was a bit slower than most, when she spoke others listened.

For instance, she would not hesitate to demand a "stop that!" to any playmate (even her older brother Steve) when and if teasing another or maybe even a defenseless pet animal got out of hand. No child would argue with her—they simply stopped what they were doing and went on to other games.

I began taking my young son, John, to play with Mazie while I worked in the pottery. My first impression of Mazie made me sure she would have a positive civilizing influence on John which turned out to be true. She taught him floor games such as cards, jacks, even paper dolls, which he promptly labeled "ol girl games" but played anyway. Mazie would just laugh at him as they became good friends who enjoyed playing together.

Later on, when they were about eight, or maybe ten years old, I was teaching dance to a group of high school girls as John and Mazie watched. Mazie came to me after the lesson and said, "teach me to do that." I knew she meant it and we began lessons once a week.

The Shaver family moved to Houston, but we kept in touch with occasional visits anytime John was with me. Later on, after my divorce, I moved to Houston with John needing to begin school there. I shall never forget the way Mazie helped John get adjusted in a new city school. We naturally chose the school Mazie went to so that he would have her to guide him.

I remember a girl, woman, of exceptional inspiration to others as she gave of herself, never whining or complaining, always ready to help another.

Chapter 25

Family ties are awesome. They are the people who can criticize, but also go through our joys and help with our heartaches. We show unconditional love in my family. Here are a few family members responses.

HAROLD "PETE" PETREE

(father-in-law)

I didn't meet my daughter-in-law until she and Jack had been married almost seven years (1975). Daniel was about 6 weeks short of his first birthday—I felt it was urgent that I meet Mazie and my first grandchild. They were living in Houston at that time—I had retired from the Air Force and was doing nothing at times. She was very busy taking care of Daniel—I was greeted very graciously. I spend 3-4 days with them. I found Mazie attractive and very capable. I assumed that she had had polio and had no problem understanding her actions.

Since that first meeting I have visited with Mazie and Jack almost every Spring. At first they thought I needed to be entertained, but I felt that just being with them and Daniel was all I needed so we settled on that. Mazie always made me feel welcome and comfortable….I have always felt that Mazie is a good wife, a doting mother (all or more attention than Dan needed), and through the years have felt I was accepted as a friend and father-in-law.

Nothing is easy for her but she just hangs in there. I have always admired her for her independence—even thought she might be having trouble doing something she wanted no help.

I'm looking forward to our relationship to continue and I hope that it will.

MARY ELLEN PETREE

(mother-in-law)

The first time we met, Mazie, I gave you only a few moments notice and didn't really have any impression of what you were like as a person. My attention was entirely on Jack and coming to terms with the surprising fact of a girlfriend in his life. To say I was pleased wouldn't be enough. I was so delighted by such a discovery, I couldn't think of anything else.

By the time we reached Houston, my curiosity about you kicked in and I wished we met in different circumstances. There was almost no chance to see you--much less get to know you. The feeling I came away with that evening was a deep regret that I had not allowed Jack to drive the car and have you sit with him. It was clear I had to do some serious changing in my behavior around Jack.

However, the opportunities to be around you, in the time before Jack told me of his wish to marry you, were almost non-existent. I was happy for both of you and had no reservations at all about the marriage, but I really didn't know you as a person. I liked you very much because you were very free and full of good humor. You seemed to me to be a real blessing in Jack's life--as a balance to his uncertainty about himself.

I was so struck by your talents for cooking and "keeping house." I was simply amazed. I knew how fortunate Jack was to have found you and loved you ---and how blessed my own life became knowing his future had you in it. I saw you teaching him such positive things as setting goals and managing money wisely. I was grateful for such good foundations to your married life.

My most cherished memory of your early years together was the tale you told of how you convinced Jack to pick up his clothes. The image I have of you meeting him at the door wearing his extra large jockey shorts is one that never fails to have me laughing. What a creative and delightful imagination and sense of humor!

Through the years, the events of Daniel's birth and the joy it brought to you and Jack holds first place as my prized memory-especially because of the long and difficult effort involved before he arrived.

Mazie, I don't think of you simply as Jack's wife now. I see you as a strong, courageous woman, full of compassion for those in need and determined to do whatever it takes to keep her marriage intact and her love alive for the future. I feel much more a mother-daughter bond now than ever before. I pray that will always be there for us and that the bond between you and Jack will grow deeper and stronger every single day.

Your son is the evidence I see of all the fine characteristics a mother can pass along to her child. You and Jack have given him a splendid foundation for his own life. It has been a joy to watch him grow to manhood and begin to see the very real treasure his parents are for him.

I believe with all my heart, Mazie, that the best is yet to come—for each of you—and for all of you.

I love you! Mazie
Mary

DEE DEE SHAVER

(my sister-in-law)

Thoughts on Louise:

Wish my fingers could "beat out" all the thoughts and feelings about this subject as fast as they can run through my head. Nonetheless, here goes.

It's so hard to believe that she's really gone. She left us with a treasury of wonderful memories and was a FIRST RATE grandmother and a wonderful mother-in-law (She was always on "my side" (can you believe that ???—lucky aren't I???) It seems that not too long after that time she was diagnosed with lung cancer, which was a crushing blow to the whole family.

Mazie was running a gift shop in town and I believe she was also involved in her work at "The Farm," in addition to maintaining her own home. She was also very involved in keeping in close touch with her son, Daniel, who lives in Florida. Somehow, thru all of this, she seemed to be holding up magnificently while tending to all of the many chores involved with her mother's care (it might have been a little easier for her to tend to Louise had she lived with Mazie, but she lived in a townhouse in another part of Sealy.)

As usual, Louise was always so grateful for anything you would do for her, and the more her illness progressed, the more docile she became. Mazie called me one day at my office. (I am retired at present. Many times I regretted the fact that I could not be of any more help to Mazie due to the situation that existed at work.) Mazie was desperately pleading for HELP.

From that point forward, Steve and I spent all of any time we had in Sealy. Louise was so thankful for her daughter's care. She proudly remarked this to me on many occasions—"Dee Dee, I don't know what I'd do without her." I truly believe that Mazie had to have had an army of angels behind her during this time, along with numerous friends in Sealy. She seemed to "breeze" right along.

About a month before Louise died, Steve went to Sealy to help Jack move Louise and her bedroom out of her townhouse and into Jack and Mazie's house. There was still a problem of what to do with the rest of the contents. The rest of the contents of Louise's townhouse had to be removed and distributed to "whomever". The following weekend, Steve, Shannon, Billy, Paulette, Steve Jr. and myself went to Sealy with a lowboy trailer and cleared out most of the rest of the contents with the exception of some items which Jack came and stored in their garage with plans for a garage sale at some other time.

I can't believe how fast Louise went after that. Miraculously to me, she never seemed to be in any sort of great pain....she just sort of drifted in to a coma and passed over into another world (a world we know is a far better place to be).

I know, though, that after you lose your last parent, you sort of feel like an orphan.... it's really a hard feeling to shake. It seems to me that Mazie and I have become a lot closer since our parents have died. (I know that Neal and Louise are proud of that.) I think that when we were raising our families there just wasn't much time (other than holidays) to get closely acquainted. Nonetheless, it was during those times that we were bonding as a family.

General thoughts:

My 3 children were born before Mazie and Jack had Daniel, and Mazie was always very interested in my children's lives. I was so thankful that the Lord saw fit to send her a child of her own, because she had so much love to give a child. She was totally devoted to Daniel, and was blessed with the sole occupation of maintaining her home and raising her child, something I always envied her for. It seems that our roles in life have reversed and I have numerous thoughts on this subject.

They say that the Good Lord never sends you any more than you can handle. Well, this is surely true. Due to the financial setback that occurred in their lives when Jack's career with Conoco was cut short during the downsizing period that all the major companies experienced in the late 80's, & early 90's. This was a difficult time for them with numerous adjustments to be made.

I think that this period in Mazie's life was probably more difficult than she, herself, could admit. However, she appeared to take it all in stride, remaining dedicated to her husband and son. I know that it's every mother's wish that their children remain fairly close by after they're grown, but here again was another "mountain" for Mazie.

While Daniel's career with Disney was a tremendous opportunity for him, I feel like it had to have created a void somehow. Nonetheless, I don't think the Lord ever removes something or someone dear to you from you immediate grasp without replacing it with something else.

This is when Mazie's gift shop in downtown Sealy developed which she seemed quite excited about. (As long as I can remember, she was always tinkering with some craft project or another—like mother, like daughter. They never ceased to amaze and amuse me with their endless original creations.)

Also, somewhere about this time was when she became involved with working out at the "Farm." This venture proved to be a financial aid to the family and seemed to be working out quite well. Unfortunately, it was not too long after this that Louise was diagnosed with cancer and things got progressively more difficult for Mazie until Louise's death.

Chapter 26

FRIENDS

"Friendship, friendship, what a wonderful friendship!"

My story cannot be completed without the anecdotes of my many friends. As stated earlier, when I began this book I wrote, called, harassed, etc. my family and friends and asked them to write or respond in some form or fashion. Some responded; some didn't. It was almost like pulling teeth to get information from some of these people. Others gave quickly and freely. So, the next chapter is devoted to other people's perceptions of and comments about me, myself, and I.

Carman told me that some of this is so "syrupy" that she isn't sure that they really know the "real" me. She wanted to edit everything. Her criteria was that whatever we put into the book had to reflect positive attributes of my personality, and tried to eliminate the "to good to be true" aspect. This is understandable. After all, if you were asked to write about someone, would you write about what a "pill" they could be or would you try to remember all the good and positive times? But, I know how hard and soul searching it was for some people to put their feelings on paper and I feel it should be all or nothing.

These friends are an integral part of my great support system. Without them and their support, it would be impossible to do what I do and be who I have become. When one is surrounded by positive "vibes" and expectations, one can't help but try to live up to these.

Friends—my family that I have picked up along the way. I hold each one dear to my heart. You will enjoy reading my friends' responses.

LETTERS FROM COLLEGE FRIENDS

PAT ROBERTS

(freshman roommate)

I have to apologize about my very tardy response to your request for info to use in your book. I have always heard that the first year of teaching is hell and I can testify to that fact; however, things are getting easier. I hope that your book is not already in print. If it is I'll just have to go out and buy it and make the time to read it. If not, here goes. (Of course, I'll still buy the book because I know it will be very special.)

As you know, I met you at Sam Houston on the first day we moved into the dorm. I had stayed awake the night before imagining what my roommate would be like. I envisioned someone fat, someone who was going to borrow all my clothes, but never pictured you. As I grow older, I realize that having the opportunity to have you in my life is a gift. I say as "I grow older" because there was not much room in my young life for people other than Robert and my parents (who I worried about constantly). It had to have been hard living with someone whose mind was usually busy with other thoughts than having fun away at college. I feel I missed out on that, but I have done very well for myself and have no regrets.

Enough about me—on the issue at hand—according to your letter, you are interested in my first responses to you. Visually, I knew that you had some sort of disability, but I was not sure what it was. It may have scared me at first because I had not thought of that. After talking with you, however, I knew that your mental abilities were OK—although you were and still are a bit of a character! Mentally, I have to admit I did not know what to do. I never really knew someone with a disability such as yours or any other kind of visible disability. Emotionally, I found myself annoyed when someone would call on the phone and say something like: "Who answered the phone? What is wrong with her voice?" Or, I found that people's questions that were annoying, but also it was that I became annoyed with having to deal with some issues that I never thought of before. Other then your disability, I liked you; however, I think you could be a little pushy.

I felt that we got along. I hope you do. I have always felt you were angry that we were not going to be roommates our sophomore year, but it was not about you. It was about the way I felt about Robert. We were almost engaged and Dianne was almost engaged to Jack. We both had one foot out the door at Sam Houston and we seemed to have the same mindset. This brings up one of your greatest attributes. That is the ability to make friends. I remember your sweet father and your vibrant and talented mother. You seem to have captured both of their good qualities. If it had not been for you, I would have probably never come out of the room and would have become more depressed than I already was at the time. It was not just because I missed Robert; I had things going on with my parents. Only children sometimes think they have the sole responsibility to set things right with everything in their houses.

One of the humorous things I remember, about the time at the dorm that you were sewing. I'm not sure you ever knew this, but I could never figure out how you could sew so beautifully and be so shaky. It bothered me though when I used all those pins. Because I was always thinking I would get up and walk around barefooted and get a pin in my foot. We had many laughs mainly about little things. Do you still have that silly looking show cap? And of course, there is always the mysterious "Oscar."

What do I think of your life? I think you can pat yourself on the back because you have surrounded yourself with goodness. You have not been given an easy road, but you have kept going. I feel God gives us all challenges in life and it is up to each of us to decide how we are going to handle them. In my estimation, you have done an excellent job. You have been a devoted mother and wife. Many people are very happy and proud to call you a friend. I am one of them.

If I could predict the future for you and for me, my scenario would go like this. You are a famous author and you are on your 99th book. We are all healthy and at peace with ourselves. We know what the really good things in life are and we get them in double dosages. That means we get to have more lunches together.

Your book is very important to me. Because I know you have a story within you.

You may use my name in your book.

SHARON WOOD LOUT

(college roommate and maid of honor)

My first recollection of Mazie was probably one, warm Autumn afternoon in the living room of Kirkley Hall at Sam Houston State College. There were many sitting areas and one area had a grand piano. That day I came in and there was new area rug that had been installed under the piano. I was looking at it. She walked over and said, "When did we get this?" Not knowing Mazie was handicapped in any way, I was a bit confused. I thought it looked really nice, but I wasn't sure if she like it. I remember looking at her and saying, "Don't you like it?" When she said, "Yes," I knew she was handicapped and I had said the wrong thing! I was embarrassed but very relieved when she looked at me and smiled and said, "Yes". She has always had a way of putting those around her at ease and she certainly did that on that day.

Later, after our first meeting over the piano rug, we met again—in the laundry room. She reminded me that one Friday night I moved her laundry out of the washer to use it. I missed her pair of maroon slacks, which I washed again with my load. She lived on the east end of the dorm and I lived on the west end. That was the night Mazie first went out with Jack. I recollect talking in the laundry room about him I believe she said she knew him and he had called and asked her out. She accepted and he has been asking her out for many years since.

Mazie's roommate or suitemate moved out to student teach, leaving a whole suite next to her available. Since my roommate and I were on the very top floor we managed to move in and occupy her adjoining suite next. It was a large corner room and very much in demand. My roommate and I lived next to her for a while until Mazie's roommate moved-on in her education. Then I moved in with Mazie.

We became very close and I spent weekends at her home in Westbury area of Houston, Jack had an old blue Chevy, which he had saved and paid for himself. We would ride to her house with him and sometimes I would go and eat on Sunday nights with the two of them. Our dormitory cafeteria was closed on Sunday nights.

Mazie's parents were always so accommodating. Her mother was a real character. She loved Johnny Carson and watched him every chance she got. Therefore, she always stayed up at night keeping herself busy. She liked crafts and, when she got started on something, she did one for everyone. She used tin snips to make pin-cushion chairs. She would cut the tin can in small strips and use needle nose pliers to bend them together and make the legs, arms, and back. Then, she put the cushioning in the chair for the pins to stick into.

She loved to sew. Not only did she have Mazie to sew for, she had a new daughter-in-law and a new grandbaby. They would come up for the afternoon to Huntsville and visit. Occasionally her dad would stop by.

One time, Mazie went home and her mother had taken the old wooden coat hangars and made neat, new padded coat hangers. They were crocheted over the old fashioned Kotex pads. Mazie went home and found her supply of Kotex used for padding in the coat hangars! I still have the ones she gave me. They have a label, which reads, "Originals, by Louise Shaver."

One weekend I visited her home, in Houston, she took me to meet her high-school friend, Judy, and her mother. Judy's mother worked at Battlestein's in Sharpstown. Judy's mother told me how much going to Sam Houston State had changed Mazie. She said she was so much more confident and her speech was so much better than when she was in high school. She was so pleased Mazie was able to go to college and attend the speech classes and therapy she was enrolled in.

In many ways, Mazie's life has not been as easy as the rest of ours. She is a very pleasant and supporting person to be with. She makes friends easy and deals with life's problems in a very sensible manner. She has the ability to fit in just anywhere. I never felt anyone treated her any differently or made her feel like she was different from the rest of us. She had so many friends in college and everyone liked her. She was always laughing and full of smiles. She had the ability to see the positive of any situation and make the very best of it. She was very optimistic always. Her difficulties she met in life she always managed to give her best. This makes her a very unusual person in the times we have today. She had very supportive parents, brother, sister-in-law, other relatives and lots of friends. She has touched many people.

As a wife and mother, Mazie was always there for Jack and for Daniel. They will always be there for her when she needs support.

HOUSTON FRIENDS

ETHEL HAMILTON

(my mother-in-law's longest and dearest friend)

I believe the first time I met Mazie was at my house. At that time my son was being transferred to Alaska since he had two weeks furlough from the Air Force. Jim and his new wife were staying with me and we decided to have a party for him. Mazie came with Jack and was introduced as "Jack's wife to be."

My impression of her, at the time, was she was a sweet girl who seemed to have some sort of handicap. I found out later she had cerebral palsy since she was a child. She didn't seem to be bothered by her handicap and was very outgoing. I admired her for that.

As the years went by and I got to know her, I loved to tease her. Sometimes she would say something that I thought was funny and I would laugh. She wanted to know why I always laughed at her. I had to make her understand that I was not laughing at her but at what she said. When she understood this, we had a lot of laughs together. Although I do not see Mazie very often, when I do, we have an enjoyable time.

I am sure that Mazie's life had to be very difficult, but no one would ever know it. She is such a brave soul. One would have to have the courage to do and try everything as normal people did. She got her degree from college, she married, had a wonderful son whom she adores. She is a homemaker, does crafts. For a time, she had a business with crafts and antiques.

I think the most memorable and touching moment about Mazie is the day she and Jack were married. At that time Mazie's walk was slow and stilted but that didn't bother Mazie, as she walked slowly down the aisle, a beautiful bride and Jack waiting for her with love in his eyes. My heart went out to her for her courage and I had to fight to keep the tears back.

Mazie is truly a brave lady and I admire her very much. She is a model example for some of us who feel sometime that our problems are overwhelming.

LINDA LINN

(friend, from Sunday School class in Alief)

February 6, 1999

First of all, I want to apologize to anyone I may offend by not using "politically correct" terms. I know I won't offend Mazie, but I'm not so sure about the rest of the world.

I was a member of the Seekers Sunday School Class, which was a part of Canterbury United Methodist Church in Houston, Texas, in 1980 when Jack and Mazie became members of that class. At that time I did no know what was "wrong" with Mazie. ….whether it was a temporary or a permanent thing. At first I thought she might be recovering from a stroke….she had difficulty speaking and she shook a lot. My experience with "handicapped" (there's that "H" word) people prior to meeting her had been limited to people with temporary handicaps such as broken bones or surgeries. At that time I had never had close contact with anyone who had a condition that wasn't going to improve. Mazie was a first for me and I didn't quite know how to deal with her.

The Seekers Class had a shared leadership which meant that anyone could teach a lesson if they so desired….no experience was necessary. One Sunday we were trying to get volunteers lined up to teach in the weeks to come and Mazie was asked if she would like to take a Sunday. Mazie commented that the only subject she knew anything about was C.P. We all said, "Fine! Talk about that."—and, she did. She got up in front of all of us and told us what her life had been like and she told it with humor and not a trace of self-pity. I learned that day exactly how to treat Mazie…just like everyone else! I have never heard Mazie say she couldn't do something—she just does it. For example, I somehow got stuck with the job of being chairperson of Canterbury's annual Halloween Carnival. Volunteers to help with the carnival were hard to come by but Mazie was on of the few who volunteered. When she and I were at the church decorating for the event, she was all over the place climbing up and down on and off chairs and stapling and taping crepe paper and other decorations to the wall. I was scared to death she would fall off a chair or staple a body part or something—(she did neither).

No longer do I consider Mazie to be "handicapped"…she

may be vocally and physically challenged to some extent, but as far as I can tell, that has never prevented her from doing anything she wanted to do—well, okay, she probably wouldn't make a very good brain surgeon, but she most likely doesn't want to do that anyhow!

Mazie is truly an amazing person with an incredible sense of humor and I consider myself extremely fortunate to have her for a friend.

PAT YOUNG

(bridge-playing friend)

My first recollection of Mazie was in 1979, shortly after I moved to Huntington Village in Houston, Texas. I met her at the Community Building where I went to play bridge. There were about 30 people there and I was eager to make friends in my new neighborhood. Mazie was very friendly and seemed to know everyone there.

After that, there was a Christmas Home Tour sponsored by the Garden Club and when I went on the tour, I met Mazie again at one of the homes. She remembered me, too. She was one of the hostesses with the Garden Club and had a big hand in doing the decorating of the home I toured.

We played bridge together after that and found that we both enjoyed crafts and ceramics. So we got together sometimes with our husbands also and had long conversations into the late hours at night. She was interested in so many things--scouting, gardening, sewing, church activities, and we had lively discussions. Jack did a lot of wooden cutouts and we brainstormed those ideas connected with woodwork. I was amazed at her ability to do so many things, which required such fine motor skills and finger dexterity, due to her unsteadiness. She was always involved in a project or cause of some kind and would devote time and effort to get the job done.

Mazie and I had a crafts booth at the annual Huntington Village Crafts Show. She knew practically everyone that came by the booth from the neighborhood and she would stand and demonstrate to the shoppers how the comforter-pillow folded up inside itself. She said that would make them sell better. She headed up her church's Holiday Craft Show and invited me to attend.

When Mazie and Jack moved away from Huntington Village, we hoped that we could still stay in touch and we did, though not frequently. We played Couples Bridge together with the Costs and the Taylors as often as we could get everyone together. One of the men, usually Gene, would get Mazie to laughing about something during the evening, and we would all get a big laugh out of it, with Mazie ending up laughing so hard, she cried. She became involved with the church in Sealy then and volunteered to lead the Youth Group activities, which Daniel was a part of. She saw where there was a need--and filled it.

She opened a business in downtown Sealy and wanted items from crafters to sell in the store. She convinced me that I should make some country lace angels to sell in the store and I did. She knew what items were popular and would appeal to the public. She told stories during that time about her experiences while being in business and most were funny stories. One was about the "flasher" who walked into the store while she was there alone. Also, the school children would stop in the store after school was out to buy necklaces with the letters in their name, which were popular at the time.

Mazie's life was very hard during that time, working long hours and on weekends to keep the business going. She also was missing Daniel, who had gone to Florida to school and to work, so being busy was a good thing then. We talked by phone whenever we could and visited the store with mutual friends.

Her mother's failing health took its toll on Mazie and she had increased health problems. Since her problems were similar in nature to what my husband had had for 25 years, she would call me, once from her hospital room, to talk about it. She always made light of it though we both knew that it was serious. She relied on her faith at these times and we tried to remain optimistic.

Mazie and Jack respected each other. Where she was lacking in physical ability, Jack would take up the slack and do what needed to be done. Mazie's mind was always racing and looking to the next steps to take.

Mazie is a very devoted mother to Daniel and takes great pleasure in his accomplishments. She adores the time she spends with him in Florida and looks forward to that time together.

Mazie has been a very loyal friend to me and we have shared our hearts about many subjects. She is a wonderful hostess and we have great times together. We've spent weekends together with our husbands at the Costs in San Marcos, and we have all six spent weekends together in Salado, talking, shopping, eating, and playing games. We have another annual trek planned to celebrate Gene's, Jack's, Mazie's, Bud's and my birthdays again in Salado in January.

Yes, you have my consent to use my name in your book.

Pat Young

JENELLE L. McARTHUR

(friend from Alief Canterbury First United Methodist Church and my adopted mother)

The year I retired was 1984 after exactly 50 years in the job market, mostly civil service. This gave me an opportunity to meet and work with many people with all kinds of backgrounds and personalities for which I was very grateful.

Moving from Seafard, Virginia to Houston, Texas was a drastic change, but I had my son's family in Houston and already established in Alief and Canterbury United Methodist Church. I give you this bit of background to establish the place I first met Mazie.

We were both new members of Canterbury but I knew when I met her she was a very special person. She is strong in her beliefs in God, herself, and her family. We worked together in the United Methodist women's Circle, craft group, Hostess Committee, Worship Committee, and other functions. Mazie and her husband, Jack, did many things for their Sunday school class and her son, Daniel's, Boy Scout troop.

You may be thinking, this sounds like what any ordinary person would do, but Mazie was so special because she had to overcome the physical disabilities of being born with CP.

Things that were maybe easy for many, took determination and effort for Mazie, but she was not a quitter and was an inventor, of sorts, to make ways for her to do the same jobs we do—but better!

I was very sad when Mazie and her family decided to move to Sealy. It left a void in my daily life that I have never been able to fill with other friendships, but our love for each other remained strong and we found time to visit and talk to each other by phone.

Sometime later, she opened an antique shop in Sealy and I had the chance to help a bit with things for the shop. Her openness made her a perfect person for this work because people instantly like her. Her mother's illness required her time, and she was again a dependable caregiver, which, to me, prepared her for her present job, which is her love and total commitment.

I treasure and enjoy my time spent with the most

remarkable person that I have met. She is a joy and a pleasure to be around and her own accomplishments are too numerous to mention so when I think of her I have a special thought and name, "Amazing Mazie," keep on course because the ring is yours for the taking!

BARB ECHOLS

(friend from Alief)

I first met Mazie about 22 years ago. I recall Rich, being outside working in the yard, and he came in to tell me to come meet our new neighbors, who were moving in across the street. I don't remember the details or exact words of our initial conversation but only an instant camaraderie with a non-working mother like I was with an almost two-year old child, going on 10, independent as they could be. And, strangely enough, the kids were only a few weeks apart in age.

Within a very short time, we discovered we all enjoyed Bridge, Rich and Jack were always working on the cars, borrowing each other tools, and Mazie and I on limited budgets cooked dinners and invited our families to partake together. We babysat during the daytime for each other, so we could accomplish tasks that would have been Herculean with a child in tow. And at night, after playing bridge, the husbands flexed their muscles and carried our sleepy-head, "dead-weight" children back across the street.

Mazie talked me into joining a ladies' bowling league, so that we could have a day a week out. The bowling alley furnished a nursery and we enjoyed a fun respite from the otherwise child-centered activities of our life. It didn't matter that neither of us was a "10-pin" star, just that we were having fun.

Not long after Mazie and I initially met, Mazie shared her story of her challenges with the effects of cerebral palsy. I don't know what prompted her to do this; maybe it was my background in special education. Anyway, it came out in little dribbles of conversation. When Mazie was born little was know about CP. In small towns like Eagle Lake, and even later in Houston, without the diagnostic knowledge we possess today, Mazie went undiagnosed. Doctors had no answers, because in many respects her involvement was less severe than those children who were institutionalized and never made it to adulthood. The symptoms were hard to attach a diagnosis to. Yet, knowing this did not ever cause me to feel sorry for Mazie. Instead I looked at her each day with growing respect for everything she accomplished. The word "No," or "Failure" were not in her vocabulary. She attended college, was an accomplished seamstress and craftswoman, had a child, even when it meant defying the doctors' advice and giving up the medication she needed to ease her tremors. She cared for her home—no maid to help her or me out, worked in the yard and gardened, cooked and most of all nurtured her loving husband and energetic son in the most devoted, caring and positive ways.

Mazie was a helpmate for me too in a very special way. The demands of my husband's job often necessitated travel, upwards to 80% of the time. Mazie was my life line to an adult world—my assurance that there were other activities that didn't include Big Bird and other Muppets with a Sesame Street address; and that intelligent conversation was still possible; and ultimately that all explanations were not followed by the question, "Why?" from a child.

Mazie also helped me to see that I was not putting my career in education on hold while I had small children at home. Rather I was providing one-to-one instruction in a home school setting for the most important students I'd ever have the privilege to educate—my daughters.

After knowing Mazie, Daniel and Jack for slightly over two years, we made a family decision to move. Our family was growing and we needed more space. As was to become typical of Houston, they flexed their annexation privileges and gobbled up our area of Alief. We didn't need city taxes or services, and we could live in Kingwood more spaciously and economically than Alief. But even then, Mazie was still a true friend. As I was arranging my belongings in my new home, she had, in true friend fashion, come behind in my old home cleaning the "dreaded" utility room.

We continued to stay in touch, sometimes with a telephone call, and at other times with a visit. Often Mazie would drop in as she traveled to and from her mom's retirement home at Lake Livingston.

Ultimately the Petrees also said good-bye to Alief for a move to Sealy. And we moved yet again to Fulshear. Jack and Mazie did their best to convince us to move to Brazos Country, but that was a little too far for Rich to commute to work. And so, on a more regular basis we were able to see each other again.

Ironically too—we consoled each other as our first born started college together, both at Texas Tech. We supported each other as our children struggled for direction in their lives, or our husbands effected career changes.

I can and always could pick up the phone or drop in and always be welcomed. And likewise, Mazie, the welcome mat and my phone number on speed dial or a collect call will never be retracted. We can pick up at a minute's notice a conversation put on hold a month, a week, or year ago.

That's the true characteristic of friendship and I truly count Mazie as one of my dearest. I love you!

FRIENDS IN SEALY

TIM WARD

(Member of my church)

My first recollection of you was when I was with Mary Emerson and she said, "Tim, you're going to have a great new worker in your church. Wish she were Episcopalian."

I was anxious to meet you because on thing we really needed in our church was eager, active people to share some of the burdens of everyday activities.

I first saw you at a United Methodist Women (UMW) meeting where it was very obvious you knew all about UMW. I was struck by your obvious disability and by the way you had overcome it. I would say my first response was emotionally—and the second one was my desire to know you better.

We had some fun times together, playing bridge, etc. but, I remember most the times at your store. I loved the handiwork displayed there, the antiques and the chance to visit. When your mother moved next door I was happy to have such a good neighbor. She must have been feeling bad even then because she didn't get out much and stayed in her housecoat. She would bake cookies and hor d'oeuvres and always have us try some out on the front patio.

When she (your mother) became so desperately ill, I felt so sorry for you because of the tremendous responsibility you were laboring under—her critical illness—your store—Daniel leaving home—Jack looking for work. It must have been a devastating time in your life and you handled it with such aplomb and cheerfulness.

I really don't know how you did—and my admiration of

you went up even more. I think you've been handed a big platter with lots of problems and I cannot think of a single person who could have handled it any better. I think you're a very strong woman with a big heart. Besides which—you're very pretty. I like and admire you, Mazie, and wish we could see each other more often.

BECKY MILLS

(Friend from church)

Several years ago, I was teaching Vacation Bible School along with Mazie. At the end of the week, we had a little program for the parents. The Sunday before, Mazie made an announcement during church of the upcoming event. As she stood before the congregation, I began to feel empathy for her but then I stopped and took a good look at her. She was not embarrassed and even though I knew it must be hard for her, she continued. I thought to myself "Why didn't someone else do the announcement?" Then I asked myself why would I think that. She obviously had never let her disease dictate her choices. Even though it would have been easier for her to let someone else make the announcement, she didn't choose to. She was not embarrassed and so since she was not, no one was embarrassed for her.

She is such a strong person; always speaking to people, always extending a friendly hand and relaying a story of interest, when it is often easier to just pass by. I feel that she is one of those people that God has truly blessed us with. She takes what life gives her and makes the best of every situation when anyone might choose an easier path. She has been an inspiration to me as I watch her work at church and within our community. She has set goals for herself and proceeds to attain those goals: never asking herself if it would be pushing herself. I often think she is the poster child for that saying, "When life gives you lemons, make lemonade." She is a sweet, brave, caring person who I feel it is an honor to know.

CLARENCE AND EVELYN McMURREY

(Friends from church)

We think we first met Mazie in 1988 when we first started attending the First United Methodist Church in Sealy. We have always considered her a good and trusting friend. We always thought her to be the same sweet and cordial person each time we came in contact with her.

We served on church committees together and through our ups and downs we were able to continue our good friendship, because of her positive attitude and her caring about relationships.

We felt Mazie to be a very caring individual. This was evident when she took a teen-age friend of their son into their home to live for sometimes. Her goodness was apparent when she gave a nice reception in her home for one or our departing pastors.

One always felt her warmth and strength of character when in her presence. We felt her to be an excellent mother to Daniel as well as a good and loving wife to Jack. We were impressed with her Christian beliefs and the way she taught her son and the way she guided him in his every day activities.

It is our belief that she has associated herself with Willow River Farms more so because of a chance to help less fortunate individuals than for the monetary reasons. Her good demeanor remained intact even in trying times in difficult situations.

We have always felt honored to be a friend of her and her

family. We felt especially honored to be invited to a recent wedding anniversary celebration with her family and many of her other friends.

You have our permission to use our name in the book. Good luck and best wishes in your writing endeavor.

JOANNE MELTON

(Friend from Church)

Met Mazie eight years ago, when I moved back to Sealy, at the Methodist church. She spoke and was very kind. I though she was a vivacious lady. Later we were putting up decorations and she climbed up the ladder in the vestibule to get down some crosses. I couldn't decide whether to offer to help her, but found out she was mighty independent. I thought she was a charming courageous lady and hope to get to know her better. It seemed she had her hand in all kinds of things in the church.

Later I played bridge with her and found she was funny and a good player with lots of friends to stand by her. I truly admired Mazie when she opened her store downtown. I knew how hard it must have been, but she did it. It was an interesting place with lots of gifts that I needed, and could have been very profitable if Mazie's mother had not been so ill. That must have been a terrible time for the family.

I feel God was working with her and led her to her new job at Willow River. She has so much love and understanding for all of her friends out there. Mazie called to ask for my help there but it appears I am going back to Gatesville for a while.

I hope you know I love you.

MARGARET COOPER

(Church secretary)

I met Mazie while working as the church secretary at Sealy First United Methodist Church. The first day I had contact with her is when she brought items for the church garage sale. I felt as if we knew each other for years. From that day on we worked on many projects together. I admire the way she could handle things. Not many things she couldn't do or try. No matter how hard it was. She has done wonders with the youth group at the church. The kids were crazy about her.

I think of Mazie a lot when I don't think I can get something done or I can't do it because she has shown me a lot of things are possible if you try.

Her life is what some would see as difficult and unusual. Mazie and her family treat it as "life as normal". She is a great wife, mother and friend. As for me, I could not ask for a better and dear friend like her. I hope I will always be a dear friend to her.

Yes, you may use my name in your book.

Margaret

JEROME AND CHERYL LOSACK
(Neighbors)

CHERYL

My first recollection of Mazie was when she, Jack, and Daniel first moved to Brazos Country. I believe that I went over to her house for our first-time meeting and we mainly discussed Alief, which was our former neighborhood as well as theirs.

214

We got along great. I believe if you can't get along with Mazie then, you probably can't get along with anybody. She is very easy to meet and get to know.

My first response visually was to see a bright, intelligent and attractive middle-aged woman with an outstanding personality. I am sure at some point I realized that Mazie had cerebral palsy but I didn't feel she was any different than myself and millions of other people.

We had a great time together doing things for the band mostly. My daughter and her son were in some classes at school together and band. Mazie and myself were excited to be in it together. She had a lot of good ideas of how to make money, etc.

The times we shared from the day we met were mostly funny. Her personality and optimistic outlook on life can't lend much to be depressed or sad about.

The only trying time I can vividly remember, she and myself and another friend went shopping one day and Mazie had to write or sign a check for her purchases. That particular day, she was shakier than other times that I had seen her. She asked me, or the clerk, to fill the check out and she signed it. I was in awe of her then and I am still in awe of her now she was not the least bit intimidated with the situation or embarrassed. Her name is written next to the word victorious in the dictionary.

She never has allowed any difficulties with cerebral palsy to give itself a chance to keep her from living her life to its fullest.

When I think of Mazie as a wife, mother, friend, worker, or any other role she may pursue, I know she has been successful and will continue to be successful. I attribute this to her optimistic but tenacious attitude to live her life to the fullest and her spiritual beliefs.

I felt her and Jack's anniversary party was probably the highlight of Mazie and her humor. She really knows how to work the crowd with her humor.

Our hectic lifestyles have kept us from seeing much of

each other. We have the relationship that if she or myself called the other in need of something, we would be there for each other.

I praise God I have met and known such a wonderful person.

JEROME

My first recollection of meeting Mazie was in the Spring of 1981. A few months after we had moved in November 1980, her, Jack and their son were on their vacant lot behind our house flying a kite.

After talking to them awhile, I went back and told Cheryl there was a couple our age planning to build behind us in a couple of years. When they did move out here, it was a while before I realized they were the couple who owned the lot behind us, but had instead, chose to buy a house down the hill already built.

We really didn't get to know each other until our children were in high school and more especially band together.

The first time I went to their house, we talked about our past, where we grew up, our size families, etc. From that time on, I began to admire Mazie for her ability to overcome her handicap and continue to move forward in life. She is a great inspiration to everyone who knows her.

As an incident would happen, be it a flood, loss of job, illness or whatever we became closer in our sharing. We shared about what we were going through at that time in our lives. They offered to help us when I lost my job eight years ago and gave us encouragement.

When I started back to achieve a bachelor of theology, Mazie said that we could come over and use their computer to type my papers for class. Little did Jack know that he would have to type the papers because I had little typing. Several times my wife, Cheryl, would go over to type my papers. The funniest thing about all of this was it was Mazie's idea for me to use the computer and it was my idea for Cheryl to do the typing.

The last time that we had a serious talk, was after her mother died and she was going through some very difficult times. I had a feeling to call her and I did. Later when I went to visit her, we sat and talked along with Jack's mother, about Mazie's fears and feelings. As usual, I came away feeling better, but I hope I was a help to her as well.

From the outside looking in, Mazie was always a giving person, especially to her son and her husband. Her priority always appeared to be taking care of their needs then and up to this day.

I feel that Mazie has had an unusual, life with difficult times, but what makes Mazie unusual is the way she handles life. She makes it look easier than I know it really is. Her strong faith in God and her positive attitude are her main tools used in her daily life.

Mazie, you have my permission to use this in your memoirs with no cost to you. Just remember me when you are rich and famous.

JEAN ADAMS

(Sealy High School drama teacher)

So, I meet Mazie! I recognize instantly that she is a sweetheart. There is something so different about her. No, it isn't the way her hands shake and it isn't the way I have to ask her to repeat herself now and then. It's something very different, very unique. I could spend some time that first year of working with Mazie trying to figure her out. (I have a hobby of trying to "figure" people out.) She was always smiling, always

217

encouraging, always helping. Why? Didn't she ever have a bad day?

Now, she and Daniel had a very normal relationship. I remember days when I thought he'd like to pull her hair out. But, then again, I get that from all of my students. That's normal, isn't it? But when she was working with me…it was nothing but optimism.

One particularly event involving Mazie sticks out in my mind. We were doing the musical "Bye Bye Birdie" and she volunteered to help make the costumes. I knew that she could sew, although I had never seen her in action. We needed about twenty double-sided circular skirts. I remember Mazie sprawled out on our theatre floor with hundreds of yards of fabric, cutting out patterns. No big deal, huh? If you've ever seen scary and pretty funny all rolled into one. I was so fascinated that she could actually cut all those skirts out, never mind sew them. But, she did. She had figured out that if she used a pair of electric scissors she could control the situation a whole lot better. My lesson from this experience: You are only as limited as your attitude. Once again, her lesson for my life wins out.

I began to figure out that Mazie's disability was her biggest asset. You see, she viewed life totally different than those of us who hadn't figured out what our disability was yet. She had been on both sides in her lifetime and she liked the positive side better. She taught me that if I had a disability, it was my attitude. She taught me to control it and not let it control me. At first glance, that may not seem like such a big deal. Think about it for a while, or better yet, try it—and you'll see just how monstrous it really is.

MILLIE FIELDS

(Neighbor, Friend)

She was and is always ready to help out when needed and in some cases before she was asked. She never asked for special treatment and was usually very understated. She was very aware of how people reacted to her 'unique' mannerisms and always tried to turn attention away from herself. She treated everyone with the same friendliness even when they seemed to shy away from her or be taken back by her abilities.

When I first was introduced to Mazie I noticed her speech and wondered what her story was. I never asked—I didn't need to. Mazie makes no excuses for her life or her choices. She lets you judge for yourself. She's too busy living with what "God gave me" than trying to explain it to others. Her life speaks for itself. I don't want to imply she's heartless or crude. She's not one to call attention to herself and I've heard her say "life's too short to worry what others think." I assume she figures if you accept her imperfections—she'll accept yours! I admire her style. I've never seen her rude to anyone. I often wondered early in our relationship if she thought I was simple-minded when I kept asking her to repeat herself as I was having difficulty understanding her speech. Now I hardly notice and when I ask for a repeat—it's usually because I'm getting deaf and can't hear well. Age tells on us all!!! I do have difficulty reading her handwriting but she does with mine also.

When we were still early acquaintances, I could see how her husband and son protected her. Maybe that was a built-in reaction to buffer her from negative results. But now that we are longtime friends I don't see that anymore. I hope that means they assume I understand their love for her and that I don't need their interaction.

BILLIE WRIGHT

(Friend from Sealy United Methodist Church)

I first met Mazie either at church or at a craft show. I bought a Christmas necklace from her which I still have. I thought she was the friendliest, most wonderful and best-natured person to be around.

Over the next years, I was around Mazie at many different places. We always managed to kid around about something. I think of her life a person with many talents. She is wonderful mother. I had the opportunity of working with her son for several summers. He is an intelligent, mature and responsible young man.

I always like being around Mazie because she is always in a good mood. Never negative about anything—just a joy to be around.

THE THERIOTS

(a family of friends)

CINDY

Dear Mazie,

I am finally writing my letter (not the first). Using this paper with the angel is on purpose because many times in our friendship years (late summer of '87) you have been there like a guardian angel, which I am very much appreciative of and I have always been in awe of you—that is after I let myself get to know the real "Mazie".

If you will recall our "beginning" was with the youth group at the First United Methodist Church of Sealy—when you were trying to start this group for the youth in our small church and you kept asking me (badgering!) to help I did not want to help you. I wanted to have my kids go and get all they could from the group, but without me! I did not know how to avoid you without it seeming like that's what I was doing. One Sunday afternoon I got a call (no caller I.D. then- insisting I come to the meeting for the youth right then. "Ooh how stubborn can one lady be!" I asked Tom my husband, as I left for the meeting. But you finally got me and over the years—like U.M.W. and working at Willow River Farm—Mazie led and I followed-which I am now and will forever be grateful. You were such a stubborn lady! My life as well as my whole family has been enriched with the friendship of you and your family—Thank you.

In the years that our lives were entwined as we took our youth group on the trips—camping or concerts or whatever—wherever you lead us whether at work with the residents of the Farm or if we were playing cards with our husbands—never considered your CP a handicap as you could do any and everything you wanted. I only noticed it because you would shake and have to try to steady yourself by putting you hand behind your head and your voice would shake and quiver when you were upset—which I am sure was often with me, but you aren't called "Amazing Mazie" for nothing!

TOM

I first met Mazie through my wife in 1987 about September after moving to a new town and knowing no one was hard. But, Mazie made it easy when we were with her and Jack, her husband. Mazie extended her hand and her friendship at the same time—a quality you don't find in most people these days. I wondered why Mazie held her neck when she spoke to a large group of strangers. I just thought she had a nervous problem—such as myself, I can't speak in public. But I guess

221

since Mazie had to cope with the illness she has had since birth. She found a way to communicate her thoughts, which is only present in a small percentage of people. I don't know if I could function in society, with a handicap, as well as Mazie has, I can only imagine, Mazie lives with it day by day and I might add, she does it with a special kind of grace.

Keep it up Mazie,

Your friend,
Tom

SHAY

I first met Ms. Mazie when I was about 8, through the Methodist Church of Sealy. Was I scared? Sure. Was I afraid of her as a person when I got to know her? Not at all. I actually began to respect her more than most adults that I've met in my 20's. She is filled with so much ambition, creation and love that its hard to be around and that not rub off on you. She has been a huge inspiration in my life and for that I am will forever be thankful.

There's so much more to Ms. Mazie than I could explain in a small letter, or even a book. She is definitely one-of-a-kind, and truly the Amazing' Mazie I know.

Love you and Thankful for everything she's shown me.

J. Shay Theriot

SHANE

My first impression of Mazie (Mrs. Petree) was a hard working person that was always positive even when faced with the difficulty of having a physical problem, which I did not understand. At first, I wondered if she could do all she thought she could. I found out she could and did. She always made me feel good about myself. I wish all the best of luck with her book and life's challenges. Thank you Mazie for being my friend.

Thomas Shane Theriot

SHANEA

When I first met Mazie I did not know what to think and I did not know anything about cerebral palsy. But after I got to talking to her, I wanted to know more about her disability. I started asking my parents' questions about the kind of disability she had and how she got it. When I learned "God gives special things to special people", I knew what it meant. She is a wonderful, fun, outgoing person who does not let her special trait stop her from doing what everyone else does. I started to see beyond the disability and inside her big heart. I now have that outlook on every one of God's creations—that is why life is such a wonderful place.

Shanea Theriot

CLOSE FRIENDS

GINNY PARKER

(Friend of my father-in-law)

I heard of Mazie for many years, approximately 21, through the glowing reports of her proud father-in-law. We had spoken on the telephone on a few occasions over the years. However, I did not meet Mazie person to person until May of 1996 on the occasion of the proud father-in-law's birthday.

My first impression was, what a nice lady and as we spent time together I knew all the glowing reports about her were truly so. While Mazie has a physical disability it has not deterred her from doing whatever she wants. I was struck by how kids immediately relate to Mazie and how easily she taught them new games and communicate with them. My grandchildren loved every minute of learning and playing those games with Mazie.

While some might view her life as a challenge, Mazie meets the challenge with cheerfulness, determination and makes everyone forget she has a challenge. Mazie has made lemonade from lemons.

We love you Mazie and you are welcome to use my name in your book.

SADIE HARRIS PHILLIPS

(close friend of the Shaver Family)

I first recall Louise, which was Mary Anna's mother, when I was a teenager in high school. I remember how vivacious and friendly Louise was. My first recollection was when Louise was pregnant with Mary Anna, as it turned out, and Steve was a little boy running around. When we lived in Palestine, we all lived out in the country and both my father and my father-in-law and Mary Anna's dad worked for the same oil company.

As far as thinking about what was her disability, I didn't really give it much thought. I had lived by a lady in Corpus who had a niece with cerebral palsy and in my head I guess I just thought that. We didn't discuss what Mary Anna's disabilities were. I didn't know that they didn't have a diagnosis. I just accepted Mary Anna like she was. She managed her own sandwiches in the kitchen and all that. She could just do about anything she wanted to do. I just took it that Mary Anna could do anything she wanted to and yet, it was a little different, but that's all right.

Mary Anna went off to college. We were thrilled when she found this fellow and he found her. Mary Anna was going to get married. We were all real happy. Then, when she was pregnant, we were all thrilled that she was going to have a baby and when we went to visit her in her home when the baby was little, she just did a marvelous job of feeding the baby and taking care of him. When Mary Anna would burp him she could really give him a good pat. She came to be a great mother.

Now that we are all much older and lost close contact I will be glad to read her book.

ROSEMARY PHILLIPS COLGIN ELLEFSON

(A dear distant cousin-in-law and a true friend)

I lived next door to your parents and I remember when Steve Mack was born. I actually baby-sat with him. Of course, I was in high school and by the time you came along, I was in college. I remember when you were born, how small you were, and how cute you were. At that time, no one knew you had any problems.

I remember thinking, then that you did have a problem with you speech and also with handling things, but I still remember how I admired your mother. It was like you said, she thought you could do everything and she expected you to do everything and we would all hold our breath sometimes that she let you do certain things. I can remember the first time I saw you try to cut something out; you were making a dress in Home Economics. But, Louise never took it away from you. She sat right there and let you do it and you did a good job of it.

I remember we tried to teach you how to crotchet. We had a lot of fun trying and that was the main thing. Like I said, you and Beth went through high school and I knew you were having a rough time at times because you did have more to overcome than others. I don't think, as usual, children are not nice and are not kind, and I know a lot of the young people were not as nice as they should have been in accepting your problem. They were too busy with their own.

I remember we were at your house one time and you were cooking or something and I kept watching to see how you were going to move that pot off that stove. But you slid it all the way across until you could get it all the way to the other side. There's also the time when I helped you find the little house that you and Jack bought. You didn't want your parents to help or to influence you in any way. This was you all's decision. Anyway, we got that done and it was a good move for you all. I think it gave you independence. But then, you had Daniel and that was another story. If I ever admired anybody was when that happened. Because we all wondered how Mary Anna was going to handle this baby.

It wasn't easy for you. It wasn't because you did not have the intelligence at all, but it was just that you had other things that I think get in your way sometimes. You had more to handle

226

than most students, but you did a good job of it. That's why I tell others that if you could go and handle it, then anyone should be able to.

Chapter 27

Dreams are dreamt and can be acted upon—
Through determination and, in my case, a great support system.

Yes I did it! Rather we did it! Accomplished what we set out to do. It only took three long, hard, argumentative years to do it. Of course, it could have been a shorter time if we had been on "Mazie time" and not "Carman time." The time that it has taken has been agonizing and has tried my patience. Really, the only obstacle I had was one of time. However, time can be overcome through patience, understanding, and endurance.

This brings back my assertion that "time," and our use of it, is when God is showing us and teaching us what we need to learn. But, I also must admit that *Mazie's Mountain* would have been finished sooner—if I hadn't had so much to say!

Again, I had to rely on my support system—Carman. However, that support system was always there, although at times, I thought I did not need it. By now, you know I like to do things myself. Yes, it is a dream come true—writing *Mazie's Mountain* in order to get "My Story" to you, dear reader.

When I was in the long process of writing this book, no one ever told me to give up on my dream. I might add, that I have found this fact to be very unusual. Don't you generally find that someone is always trying to hinder or even stop you from going for your dream? Daddy did not step on my dream when I was nineteen and I expressed my desire to write a book. Do you remember? Now, I am in my mid-fifties and my family and friends have also supported this dream—or maybe they just know Mazie. They know that whatever I have for a goal I keep working until I accomplish it or find the help I need to get to it. In this instance, it took both, my support system and me. This was just one more mountain I was able to climb. Finally…..

I have a lot of life left. Where will I go next? What is the next mountaintop for me to climb? I know that whatever comes it will have those awful valleys. And, I know that to be able to grow I need to keep climbing. Maybe the valleys won't be so deep from now on. But, come what may, God is my refuge and Jack, my family and my friends are my support.

Don't let anyone stop you from dreaming or reaching the mountaintop. Soar with the eagles and dare to fly. Let the winds, ones family and friends, support your wings and God will give you the speed and endurance to accomplish your dreams.